disse
tous.

THE PRETTIEST HORSE IN THE GLUE FACTORY

THE PRETTIEST HORSE IN THE GLUE FACTORY

COREY WHITE

A MEMOIR

HAMISH HAMILTON

an imprint of

PENGUIN BOOKS

HAMISH HAMILTON

UK | USA | Canada | Ireland | Australia
India | New Zealand | South Africa | China

Hamish Hamilton is part of the Penguin Random House group of companies
whose addresses can be found at global.penguinrandomhouse.com.

Penguin
Random House
Australia

First published by Hamish Hamilton, 2019

Cover design by Adam Laszczuk © Penguin Random House Australia Pty Ltd
Cover images: horse head © yusuf madi/Shutterstock; horn © Mila_Endo/Shutterstock
Typeset in Adobe Caslon Pro by Midland Typesetters, Australia
Printed and bound in Australia by Griffin Press, part of Ovato, an accredited
ISO AS/NZ 14001 Environmental Management Systems printer

A catalogue record for this
book is available from the
National Library of Australia

ISBN 978 0 67007 934 6

penguin.com.au

MIX
Paper from
responsible sources
FSC® C009448

For Sophie

Leopards break into the temple and drink all the sacrificial vessels dry; it keeps happening; in the end, it can be calculated in advance and is incorporated into the ritual.

Franz Kafka, *The Zürau Aphorisms*

1

My father taught me to kill. In balmy Brisbane nights, on our front lawn and in our backyard, we kill cane toads together. We smash them with cricket bats, we squish them with hammers. We crush them with our feet, we pelt them at brick walls.

At first I felt sorry for the toads. Now I don't care. My father tells me they're pests. The Government brought them from Hawaii to eat cane beetles but they found easier prey. They spread, killing native wildlife and people's pet dogs. We're fixing the Government's mistake.

One night after we have killed cane toads, we lie out on the dewy grass, looking up at the stars.

My father drinks a beer and smokes as I lie on his chest, feeling safe.

'How many stars are there?' I ask.

'Nobody knows. Pretty cool, hey?'

I nod, bewildered.

'Heaven's up there too,' he says, cigarette wagging in his mouth. 'If you're good, you'll go there.'

I smell the cane toad guts on my fingers. 'Do cane toads go to Heaven, Dad?'

He pauses. 'If they ask Jesus to forgive their sins.'

My father mentions sin a lot. I am five and I don't quite understand what it is. It seems very grown-up and important, like *tax* or *America*.

'What's sin?' I ask yet again, feeling as incapable as when I try to say *hospital* properly.

'Sin is doing what goes against God's wishes.' Out of the corner of my eye, the little sun of my father's cigarette glows. 'Drinking like Daddy is. Smoking like Daddy is. Every person sins, but Jesus died for us so we could be forgiven and have eternal life.'

I savour the enormity of his pronouncement.

Then I feel clever. 'What if you don't have any sins?'

'You're innocent now,' he tells me, 'but one day you'll sin.'

That's one of my few early memories. I forget more than I remember and what I do remember are shredded vignettes, bad student films, as if I were born with a reverse dementia which gradually lifted. Things before are a muddled chronology. A great veil cloaks the years.

I lie in the dark counting the letters. Sin. S-I-N. Three letters. Three. 3. Sin, sin, sin. I like that it is symmetrical, you can take the *s* and put it on one side then while the *i* is in the middle you can give half of it to the *s* and half to the *n*.

I think I am four when I first realise that I am alive. I am hiding in a bush in our front yard, playing with Matchbox cars in the fine grey dirt. I watch a man walk his dog on the footpath. The dog, intrigued by something, cuts across his owner's path then darts behind his legs and back in front, binding then toppling him. 'Shit!' yelps the man as he falls face-first onto the concrete. I giggle, enchanted by the misfortune.

We live in a Housing Commission estate in Caboolture, a pale brick house in a long street of pale brick houses with fences of tessellated wire diamonds.

Cockroaches scatter over the pink kitchen bench, a vanishing constellation of brown bodies in the morning sun. I decide against Vegemite toast for breakfast. Instead I go to the fridge and take a good long swig of my mother's Coke.

I can't remember any of my birthdays. No, I can. McDonald's. Pancakes. Too many to eat but I always got them. The little moon of butter that never disappeared.

———

My father bounces, in aqua shorts and no shirt, his skin warm caramel. Above the trampoline the world is lilac but for the orange sun, which is abandoning the sky, and we are floating and falling in unison. I love him, nothing is more delightful than being with him, I want to be closer to him than his moustache.

'I don't want to go to kindergarten,' I announce, jumping hard to try to throw my father off-balance.

'Give it a try, son.'

'It's shit.'

I love to jump. My mother tells me when I was three I leaped off the roof of a house and through the roof of a cubby house. Everyone raced to me, thinking I'd died, but I lay in the wreckage giggling. I'd been a very mischievous toddler. Apparently my parents had to tie me to my high chair to stop me from wandering off.

I believed these stories, these legends. Nothing could hurt me. I was invincible.

My father is wonderful at drawing; once he drew a tiger on a beer coaster with a biro and it looked like a photograph. I keep it in my pillowcase and admire it often. I hope one day I'll be able to draw as well as him. He tells me I am destined for great things. He knew it before I was even a twinkle in my mother's eye. When I build starships out of Lego he kneels down in awe and calls me *genius*. And because it is him telling me, I believe it completely.

———

I am a one-boy public relations operation for my father, shouting out press releases to anybody who will listen.

'You know my dad jumped off the Townsville Bridge and lived,' I shoot at Linda, one of my mother's friends.

'Wow!'

'Nobody has ever jumped off the Townsville Bridge and lived except Dad.'

'Gosh,' she says, lighting a cigarette. 'Do you know why he jumped?'

I'm stumped because that's all the information I've been given to pass on.

I am not close to my sisters Belinda and Rebecca. To me they exist simply to reduce the amount of ice cream I get at dessert. And they are only my half-sisters; we have different fathers. Unlike mine, their faces are speckled with freckles which I think look like fly shit. I've never seen fly shit but I think that's how it would look.

We fight a lot. For instance, my sister Belinda is always smelling her fingers for some reason and it makes me sick. I tell her how I feel about her finger-sniffing and she tells me it's a free country. It's embarrassing when we go shopping and she's holding her hand to her nose like it's a bouquet of roses.

Rebecca is stuck-up. She's prettier than Belinda and knows it. She is good at school and dances and plays netball.

Jacinta is my real sister. My father is her father too. She's four years younger than me – she's only two. I don't mind her.

I am my father's favourite because I am his son. Rebecca and Belinda complain that I am my mother's favourite too. I see no problem with this state of affairs. I *am* better than them. It seems only natural.

I play our Sega constantly. I want to be the greatest player in the world. The feeling of my mother and father watching me, yelping when I do something, makes my tummy feel like a smile. I sit in the lounge room until my mother forces me to turn it off for *Neighbours* and *Home and Away*.

'Gimme a go,' Belinda says, sitting down beside me.

'No.'

She leans over and wrenches the controller from my hand. I punch her in the breast, the place I've learned is the best target. She slaps me in the face.

'Dad!' I yell. He appears. 'Dad, Belinda stole the controller.'

He removes his belt and Belinda pleads that she is sorry.

'Stand,' he commands. She drops the controller in my lap and rises. 'Come here.' Belinda goes to him. He hugs her into his chest, locking his arm around the back of her neck. Then he brings the belt down on her backside, once, twice, three times. He keeps going. I lose count. She screams and screams until the screams become one scream. 'Don't,' he puffs, 'fuck with my son.'

I watch his arm release her neck and Belinda collapse to the floor gurgling, a broken water bubbler. He kicks her in the ribs and she groans. 'Go to your room.'

Belinda crawls down the hallway, her crying fading like an ambulance siren.

'Slut!' I shout after her. My father pats my head.

'Barry,' slurs my mother from the couch. 'That was too much.'

———

He hits my mother, he hits my sisters, but he does not hit me. I am special, his favourite. I am beloved.

My father takes me to the movies often. We sit in the cool darkness munching on popcorn and slurping frozen Coke. Once we go to see *Casper the Friendly Ghost* and I become obsessed. I put a sheet over my head and try to scare everyone. I'm unhappy that there are no white sheets in our house but I make do with pink.

'Boooooooo!'

'I know it's you, Corey,' Rebecca deadpans.

My little sister Jacinta, who is three, giggles like an idiot.

I'm upset they're not scared so I sit on my bed and think. I realise for me to be a proper ghost I'm going to have to be dead.

I find my father on the couch watching TV. 'Dad, I need you to kill me so I can be a ghost.'

'Son, I can't do that.'

'Come on, Dad,' I say, leaping on his lap, 'I love you, please kill me.'

'I'm not killing you, Corey.'

I kick away from him, furious. I decide when I grow up I want to die.

My Uncle Wayne is babysitting me while my parents go to watch Rebecca and Belinda in a dance performance. He is fat with blond curly hair, wearing a maroon shirt and navy-blue ruggers. His face is all red and stretched and he has a pig nose.

'Goodbye,' my parents call as the front door shuts behind them.

'Corey, come here,' Uncle Wayne says.

I sit beside him on the couch. 'Yes, Uncle Wayne?'

'Do you have a doodle?'

'Of course I do! I'm a boy.'

'Why don't you show me?' I pull my pants down and flop my doodle out. Suddenly I feel awkward. Uncle Wayne isn't saying anything.

'Are you okay?' I ask.

'I'm great,' he says. 'Do you want to see Uncle Wayne's doodle?'

'Nah, I want to play Sega.'

'You can play Sega after you see it.'

I see his hand dig into his pants and he pulls out his pale, sausage-looking doodle.

'Woah, that's big!' I say, impressed.

'Do you reckon your penis can get bigger?'

'I don't think so.'

'Go on,' he says encouragingly. 'Try to make yours bigger.'

'I don't really wanna.'

'That's okay, I'll do it for you.' He reaches over and fiddles with my doodle. It stays small.

'Do you wanna touch my doodle?'

'Not really.'

'That hurts my feelings,' he says.

Reluctantly, I lean over and hold his doodle like a sausage. I feel his hand on mine, pushing it down and pulling it up.

'I don't wanna do this. Can I play Sega?'

'No, no, let's do this for a while,' he says gently.

'I wanna play Sega. This is boring.'

'Just do this and then you can play Sega.'

My tummy boils. I don't like this, so I pull away and stand up.

'Where are you going?' Uncle Wayne asks.

I throw open the front door and bolt out. I'm going to get on the roof. I clamber up onto the bin and then onto the garage roof.

'Corey?' I hear Uncle Wayne say, wandering out the front door beneath me.

'What are you doing?' he says, looking up at me.

I feel hatred. 'I'm on the roof, derrbrain, to stay away from you!'

'Please come down, I'll give you ice cream.'

'I don't want your fucking ice cream, cunt.'

He looks around. 'You're not going to tell your dad about this, are you?'

'Yes, I will. I tell my dad everything. He's my best friend.'

'Shit,' he mutters.

I don't know why I'm angry. I also need to wee. The two things merge in my mind. I start trying to wee on Uncle Wayne. He jumps back. I push harder and lean back trying to land the arc on his head.

'You sicko!'

I cackle, the wee cascading through the dark sunshine of the late afternoon. Some of the wee splashes his shoulder.

'Yuk! You're gonna pay for this!'

He starts to walk up to the bin. Evidently, he's trying to climb onto the roof.

I run to the edge of the corrugated iron and kick at his head and he topples backwards off the bin onto the grass. His face curls and he starts crying. 'That was mean, Corey. You've hurt me!'

'Fuck off, go away!'

He stands, tears streaming down his face. 'Please don't tell your dad about this.'

'Oh, I will be telling Dad about this,' I say, still not quite knowing why.

He turns around, unlatches our gate, walks out onto the footpath and starts jogging down the street. I sit down on the roof and watch him recede into the distance.

Eventually, I climb down off the roof, go inside the house, lock all the doors, grab a kitchen knife and start playing Sega. If Uncle Wayne comes back, I'll stab him.

A few hours later, I hear the front door click open.

Mum and Dad walk in and ask where Uncle Wayne is. I say casually, 'We played video games and he touched my doodle.'

'What?' my mother says.

'We played video games and Uncle Wayne touched my doodle. It was yucky.'

I explain the situation.

'Are you sure you're telling the truth, Corey?' asks my father.

'Yes. We touched each other's doodles. His was big.'

My father punches a wall. 'He's a fucking paedo!'

'Paedo!' my mother barks towards Heaven.

'What's a paedo?' I ask.

'A paedo is a paedo!' comes my mother's crying tautology.

I don't know what the big deal is. I tell them I'm okay, that Uncle Wayne didn't hurt me or anything. I just feel a bit weird.

Holding my hand, my father announces we are going to find the rock spider. It seems like a strange time to go find a spider but I don't argue.

We drive to Uncle Wayne's house, about an hour away. I sit in the back seat with my sisters in silence. When we pull up, my father says, 'Stay here,' before opening the door and marching into Uncle Wayne's house, my mother following him.

The next thing I know, my mother is shaking me. 'Wake up, Corey,' she says. We are back at home. My father picks me up and carries me inside to my room.

'I love you, son,' he says, as he tucks me into my bed.

'I love you too, Dad.'

I never see Uncle Wayne again.

I watch *Captain Planet* and I want to save the world just like him. It feels as though I am waiting for time to pass until something enormous happens. When I play Sega, I imagine I am training for the army.

My father lets me have sips of his beer at night 'to kill the worms'. I suck greedily at the brown bottle until he gently takes it from my hands. I don't like the taste – it reminds me of how the toilet smells after he uses it – but I always say yes; to me it is a magic potion that, with each sip, brings me closer to being him.

———

My father is very smart. He knows that the capital of Papua New Guinea is Port Moresby. He gets most of the answers right on *Sale of the Century*.

He tells me funny jokes. My favourite is, 'What's Bruce Lee's favourite drink? Wataaaaaaaaaaaaa!' accompanied by karate hands.

His favourite number is seven and I tell everyone it's my favourite number too but really my favourite number is three. I like three because zero plus one plus two equals three. No other number is like that.

My father loves chess. He sets up a little wooden board on the kitchen table and teaches me the rules. He tells me about the greatest chess player who ever lived, Bobby Fischer. He was American and he was the world champion, single-handedly defeating the communists.

I don't quite understand the rules of chess. The horses move in L-shapes. I look at the board in wonder. There are so many possible moves. What is the best one? I play my father.

'How do the horsies move again?'

My father corrects me. 'They're called knights, not horsies, and they move in an L-shape.' He shows me on the board. 'See?'

'Yep.'

He beats me.

———

'Where does evil come from?' I am sitting on the train with my father playing our game of exploring the world.

'The Devil whispers into our hearts.'

'Why don't people ignore his whispers?'

'They can't tell it's the Devil.'

I drink in my father's anger, see how it makes him glow and other people cower, and I repeat it.

I punch my mother in the stomach and call her a stupid slut. I chase my sisters around the house with cricket bats and knives and, one time, blinded by fury, I pursue them with a headless Barbie doll.

There is something enormous in me. A golden gunshot waiting to enfold the world. I am a sky and a house and a hug.

I am running after Rebecca with a knife. She pleads for me to stop in ragged breaths, leaping over the neighbour's fence.

'Don't ever turn off my Sega ever again ever,' I shout from our side of the fence.

'I won't,' she promises.

'You better not,' I yell, jogging inside to keep playing.

I believe my body is invincible.

I lie down in the grass and let the green ants bite me, to see how much pain I can handle.

I believe I have the strongest, most marvellous legs in the world. I lie on my back and rearrange my room by pushing furniture around with my feet. I take long baths and admire the musculature of my quadriceps and calves. When my mother's friends come over I wear short pants and strut around like a proud rooster. Nobody ever notices, though, and inwardly I'm saddened that I never hear the words, 'What magnificent legs Corey has.'

My parents gave me two middle names: Boden Bonham. Boden is what my mother called her first, miscarried son; Bonham is the surname of the Led Zeppelin drummer who choked to death on his own vomit. It's hard to think of bleaker choices.

My father tells me I was named Corey because it means *the chosen one*. Because of my name I will do great things. I wonder why everybody doesn't just name their child Corey. Then everybody would be the chosen one and do great things.

'What do Rebecca and Belinda mean?' I ask, hopping aside as Dad fixes himself a devon and tomato sauce sandwich.

'Nothing special,' he says.

My mother had grown up in a solid middle-class family. Her father was a bank manager back when that was a prestigious position. Nana worked in Myer.

My father's upbringing was hellish. His father had served in

World War II in New Guinea and Borneo. His mother, Meta, was schizophrenic. His father abandoned his family, leaving Meta to raise six children by herself.

As a child, I did not know this. All I knew was his fury, how he made people cower.

My father takes me to the pub where he drinks beers and bets on horse racing. He speaks of systems, quinellas, exactas, trifectas, quaddies.

It is our special paradise. Most of all I adore the smoke, the way it unfurls in the air like ghosts from cigarettes. I love the silence of the men with the occasional eruptions of hope.

'You little beauty!' my father yells when his horse is doing well. 'Go you good thing!'

When he loses, he yells, 'Fucking cunt!'

We sit inside the pub for hours. At first it's exciting but before long I get bored. 'Can we go home, Dad?'

'Just one more race,' he says, five times.

The pub is filled with old men. Their white beards are stained with nicotine. They have dirt under their fingernails and wear faded denim jeans and paunch-stretched singlets. My father wears thongs with white soles and black straps and, as he dances around the pub willing the horses to triumph, his thongs seem to be clapping for the horse to win. He sinks into moroseness or glides with mania. The men yell for luck, crying 'Jesus' and muttering 'fuck'. They call the horses and dogs 'geniuses' or 'failures'. It feels as if we're a community. When somebody wins big they buy other men beers and they buy me a raspberry cordial.

When a race is being run, when the tension is highest in the room, when everything is deathly silent, I like to look around at the faces of the men and see the emotion in their wide eyes. I can't put it into words, but it makes me feel special, like the night before Christmas. It's also air-conditioned, relief from the sweltering heat outside.

Sometimes my father intuits that I should select the horses for his quinellas and trifectas, a task which I approach with great solemnity.

'Three looks good,' I say with a false confidence. 'Three's always a goer,' I mimic.

'All right,' he says. 'What else?'

'Nine has to be in there too,' I prophesy, but the only reason I've selected it is because it's three multiplied by three.

'Okay.'

I mull the third number. I look at Dad gazing up at the TV. I think he'd like me to say seven, his favourite number. I don't like seven, though. It's not a very beautiful number. I say it anyway because I don't want to hurt his feelings. 'Seven.'

'That's Daddy's favourite number,' he says, marking the betting slip in the pretty blue ink of a biro.

'Yep.'

He gets up and places the bet then returns.

The trifecta doesn't come in.

'Fuck,' I say, slamming my fist down on the table like him. 'Bloody crook.'

When my father has finished losing money we walk to the bottle shop next door. He buys a slab of beer and we make the kilometres-long journey home. He had promised to carry me on his shoulders but I have been usurped by the carton of beer. I trudge sullenly beside him, jealously glaring at the cardboard box which has stolen my place on his shoulders.

My fish Leonardo dies. He's on his back, floating, with a long trail of brown stuff behind him.

'He's just doing a big poo,' my mother reassures me.

'He's dead.' I know my mother is lying. I cannot prove it but I yell for her to stop.

My father grabs her by the throat. 'Don't lie to our son, you whore.'

'I'm sorry, Barry.'

'Don't apologise to me,' he spits, 'apologise to Corey.'

She gazes at me with watering eyes, neck deep red. 'I'm sorry, Corey.'

'Tell him the truth,' my father commands.

'Leonardo died. Your fish is dead.'

I don't like that my father is choking my mother. 'Awesome,' I burst out, willing him to let go.

I'm setting a trap for my sisters. It's a nail through a plank of wood which I carefully place at the back door so when I call them they'll tread on it and scream in agony.

First I have to test that my trap works.

I place my foot on the nail to evaluate its sharpness. Pressing down, I feel the sole of my foot grow tight from the tension. And then there is pain. I howl and lift my foot up, the piece of wood rising with it.

'Ahhh!' I scream.

My father appears. 'What have you – shit!' He sweeps me off my one leg, storms through the house cradling me and the wooden plank in his arms. We reach the bathroom and, still holding me, he leans over the bathtub and turns on the water with one hand. He lowers me in onto my bottom and unfolds my legs like origami, my blood transforming the water pink.

I'm dumbstruck that I can be hurt like this. I lose a little faith in the power of myself.

One afternoon when I get home from preschool, my father isn't there.

'Where's Dad?' I ask my mum, who's smoking a bong and watching *Play School* with Jacinta.

'He's in jail.'

Jail? Isn't that where bad people go? 'But Dad didn't do anything!'

My mother doesn't answer and I shiver, afraid my father isn't home to protect us. My mother and my sisters seem unconcerned about the safety implications of his absence. 'What if somebody breaks into our house and tries to hurt us?'

'We'll be okay,' my mother says, swigging from a two-litre bottle of Coke before snapping off a row of Cadbury fruit-and-nut chocolate and popping it in her mouth. Burping, she smiles. She has her legs stretched out on a foot cushion, newly painted toenails gleaming red.

That night I try to sleep but the darkness is too much. I climb into bed with my mother and pretend she is him.

I wonder what jail is like. I soon find out when my mother takes us on a long car ride to visit him at Wacol Prison. Outside, the landscape is dry and dead.

When we walk into the covered visitor's area he is sitting at a metal table. Spread out in front of him are several blocks of chocolate and a big packet of Smith's salt and vinegar chips. Other men are sitting with their families at tables. One man is making fart noises with his armpit and hand to the delight of his children.

'I'll be home soon,' my father promises.

With my father gone, I carry on the war against the cane toads alone. I am Luke Skywalker and they are stormtroopers. Jacinta tries to join in once but I push her away. This is *my* quest. And when I impale toads with a cricket stump or crush them with a light purple brick, I imagine there is a camera filming me and my father is watching me, proud.

Some nights I drag my blanket and a pillow into my wardrobe and sleep there because, if a murderer breaks into our house, they won't see me. I'm always thinking of plans to escape danger. I watch *Home Alone* on repeat for strategies.

Things change after my father goes to jail. My mother makes me go to preschool every day. I have to go to sleep at 8 o'clock. She even tells me not to swear because good boys don't swear.

'Fuck off,' I tell her.

'That's it,' she declares. 'I'm washing your mouth out with soap.'

'Shut up, slut,' I say, trying to focus on *Alex the Kidd*, the Sega game I'm playing.

She marches me to the laundry and washes my mouth out for swearing. When she finishes, I spit and sputter the soapy water into the basin. 'Wait until I tell my father about this!' I scream. 'You're gonna pay, slut!'

'Get back here!' my mother says, moving to seize me again, but I'm already out the back door, sprinting into the yard, running through my own dribble.

'Corey!'

I skid, turn to look at my mother, yell, 'You're a fat cow, you can't catch me!'

I share a birthday with my mother. 'You were the best birthday present I ever got,' she says. I wish I shared a birthday with my father. I have her deep brown eyes but I wish I had my father's hazel eyes. His eyes are better. People say I have puppy dog eyes but I don't want puppy dog eyes.

I lived in an eternal apocalypse. I always awaited the Day of Judgement. Jesus would come and take all the good people up to Heaven, and my father would never ever go to jail again.

In time, the fantasy lost its content but the form of it remained within my mind. I continued to believe that someday, somehow, everything would turn gold. I was anesthetised to suffering by the assumption there would be a coronation far into the future.

All I had to do was wait for the golden future. In the future my father would come home and Jesus would return; the twin dreams were near.

Maybe it was better this way. In delusion there is safety.

When my father returns from jail I shriek and run into his arms. He is leaner, browner, more beautiful. He has on a crisp pair of light-blue denim jeans, sandshoes and a white singlet underneath a red flannelette with the sleeves rolled up to the elbows. His light brown hair is neatly combed to one side. He is the handsomest man in the world, and I breathe in his smell, the one I love, of Brut and tobacco.

'Listen to your mother,' my father says deferentially. 'She knows what's best for you. It's bedtime.'

I do as my father says, surprised at his tenderness to my mother. He's changed.

Later that night, I get up and tiptoe to my mother's bedroom to sleep beside him. When I open the door, my nostrils fill with the smell of beer and sweat. My father is on top of my mother, one shadow conquering another. One shadow hissing, one shadow sobbing.

'Please stop,' my mother begs, but the shadow swallows her mouth.

I back away from the door, from the man who made me, who hissed me into existence.

2

My mother doesn't speak of sin. She smokes bongs, listens to Fleetwood Mac, drinks Bundaberg Rum with Coke, masturbates in her bed with the door closed.

She tells me that I'm her darling, her favourite, but I can't tell the others. My specialness is a secret. But at seven I can't keep secrets, especially during fights with my sisters. When Rebecca or Belinda try to play video games with me or we battle for the last sip of Coke or final inch of Nutella, I gloat about my mother's love.

'I'm Mum's favourite! She loves me more than you.'

They always run to her and ask if it's true.

'I love all you kids equally,' she insists, hugging them close to her and widening her eyes at me over the top of their heads, putting a finger to her mouth.

———

My mother is coaxing me to eat my vegetables but I don't want to. I have noticed that food tastes better when I am starving. I like the growing dizziness of hunger. It is a game, to see how long I can resist. It makes me feel strong to not need anything.

I apply the same theory with water. When I play outside on the trampoline I jump and jump until my mouth is a desert, then drag myself wearily to the garden hose and guzzle water until my belly hurts.

'Come on,' my mother says at dinner one afternoon. 'Eat your veggies.'

'No.'

She stabs some broccoli with my fork. 'Come on, eat your veggies so you can grow up big and strong.'

I punch her hand. 'Fuck off.'

'Leave him alone,' bellows my father from across the room.

'He needs to eat his vegetables.'

Suddenly my mother flies backwards into the glass door, sliding into a seated position. She ducks her head but my father already has her by the hair. He knees her in the face then pushes her back up against the glass with his hand gripping her throat. He punches her in the stomach and she cries out.

Twisting free of my father, she flees into the kitchen. He chases after her. 'Come back here, cunt.'

She sprints into the lounge room then back into the kitchen, my father in hot pursuit. Realising she can't outrun him much longer, she dashes down the hallway and locks herself inside the sanctuary of the toilet. From my chair, I watch my father launch himself at the door, over and over.

Finally, he breaks through.

Guttural cries. The rabid cadence of fists hitting flesh. Mashed potato on my plate. Rebecca clutches my hand, says, 'We have to get out of here.'

With Belinda and Jacinta in tow, we run barefoot over the bitumen and dry grass and sand to Suttons Beach and dive into the water. I punch and kick the waves, imagining I can destroy the ocean. I karate chop the cresting water and pretend it breaks because of me.

We return to our house hours later, our feet speckled with sand, our bodies perfumed with the sea.

I can't remember if my father was penitent or if he was even home. The toilet smelled of blood for days.

People ask me now how it was to witness my father do these things. I lie and say I was scared of him. I wasn't. He never touched me. I was his son, cherished, granted immunity from brutality.

The truth is that I admired my father. I never tried to protect my mother or my sisters. I was complicit in the fury he heaped on them.

I went further: I copied him.

I hate going to school.

I watch the port rack knowing how easy it would be for a thief to steal from it. It causes me unbearable anxiety. I bite my lip three times on the left, three times on the right and three times in the middle, but it does nothing for the razor feeling in my stomach. I repeat my lip ritual twice more, yet I still feel edgy.

I am different to other children. I want to kill them, conquer their laughter. They only want to climb monkey bars. I look at a kid, Alex, next to me, and I want to choke him. I like it best when I'm by myself.

I loathe the presence of other children. Their snotty noses. They are beneath me.

At lunch time I sit by myself in the sandpit and build castles.

After lunch, the teacher shows us pictures of animals and the class has to shout the name of what is on the card. What idiot doesn't know a dog is a dog?

The other reason I don't like school is because it's hard to hear what people are saying.

My mother takes me to get hearing aids fitted. After the beeps and boops, the woman fits my ears with a cold pink putty.

My hearing aids come a few weeks later. When I put them in, I can't believe how much sound I can hear. I don't like them, though. They mean something is wrong with me. I'm not perfect any more. I'm like flat Coke.

When school ends, I sit out the front and wait for my father to arrive.

He strolls in, an hour late. I uncross my legs, get up from the footpath, and walk to him.

'How was your day?' he asks.

'Boring. I hate it here.'

When we get home, I tell my mother that I'm not going back.

'It's good for you, Corey,' she insists.

'Michelle,' says my father, 'he's too smart for the place. It's a waste of his time.'

The next morning, while Rebecca and Belinda rush off to school, I sit in the lounge room playing Sega.

My mother quibbles at first, but after my father convinces her I'm too smart for school she goes along with it. Each morning I wake up and watch cartoons. I play video games. I go outside and jump on the trampoline. I read books and picture all the words living inside of me forever. I dream of reading all the books in the world.

I adore my Little Golden Books. Nothing pleases me more than their shiny golden spines, how they shimmer in the sunlight as I lie on the trampoline. I read the dictionary a lot. Each day I discover new words like *magnificent* and *synchronised*. Words are jewels, magic incantations. Deep down inside me, I believe you can read words aloud and become rich or handsome or safe. I am storing up these words for some great purpose in the future.

'What do you call a pharaoh honking in traffic?' grins my mother.

'What?'

'A tooting car man.'

I laugh and laugh.

She sighs, says softly, 'I love you more than all the gold in Egypt.'

———

I shower with my mother, fixated on her furry vagina. I watch the water dripping off the ringlets, fascinated.

'You came out of this,' she tells me.

'Huh?'

'When Mummy gave birth to you, you came out of her vagina.'

I think it looks rather unhealthy.

I love when my mother tickles me. She scoops me up, drapes me in her lap and holds my hands.

'Round and round the mulberry bush, like a teddy bear,' she teases, walking her fingers slowly up my forearm. I giggle knowing what's coming. I beg her to stop but I want her to go on.

'One step,' she taunts, sending shiny dread through my body. 'Two step.'

'No, no, no!'

'Tickle him under there!' she hoots and plunges her hand into my armpit. I writhe with laughter as her fingers dart over my neck and stomach.

'No, Mummy, no!' I howl with happiness.

As an adult, I can't stand people touching my belly button. Visions come, of a hand descending down my chest, its fingers marching across my body.

If people graze my belly button with their fingers during sex, my hands curl into fists. I don't even like touching my belly button myself, and there have been times when it has resembled a dryer's lint filter.

My mother slows the car down beside a woman pushing a trolley filled with groceries along the footpath.

She leans across me and yells, 'Oi!'

The woman looks up, startled, her face quickly contorting in recognition.

'Suck my clit!' my mother hollers, flooring the accelerator, as I watch the woman flip the birds in the rear-view mirror.

'What's a clit?' I ask my mother later.

She lifts up her sarong, pushes her black underwear to the side.

'This is Mummy's clit,' she says, flattening the mat of her pubic hair and pointing at a vertical pink almond. 'The man in the boat.'

My mother lies on her bed, dress hitched up to her belly and a hand between her legs, middle finger down and wriggling. Her legs tremble, and I can see her eyes scrunched in pleasure.

Bethany's teeth are sharp little triangles tinged black. She's dirty, like me. She lives next door and I decide I want to fuck her.

'Let's have sex,' I whisper to her as we play with cars in the dirt.

I lean towards her and kiss her on the lips. She puts in some tongue, and I touch it with mine, tasting her sweet wet mouth.

We go inside to lie in her parents' bed and we have what we think is sex. We pull the blankets over us. I rub my penis on her belly for a few seconds, breathing heavily the way my father does, whooshing and hissing. I like it, the look of our bare bodies, the feeling of our clothes gone.

She grabs my hand and rubs it on her vagina.

From behind us, I hear my father say, 'Oi, what are you doing?'

I turn around to face him while Bethany pulls her underwear up.

'Oi, don't do that,' he says to me.

'I'm sorry,' I say.

'No more of that, you hear?'

Sometimes now, as an adult, I feel painful sensations in my body of someone squeezing me around my stomach from behind, their fingers hooking my belly button. It's hard to breathe and something invisible drives me down, enveloping me.

I want to scream, but I am completely immobile. I lie still, my body limp, and when I try to get out of bed, I can't move my legs. I can't move them no matter how hard I try.

I go inside myself, searching for explanations. I think back to when I was a child, sort through every scene that comes to my mind, trying to find the one that explains this.

Nothing.

I can feel fingers scraping my belly button again. I growl into the pillow in agony.

My mother is always vanishing. She leaves us alone in the house and Rebecca goes mad with power, bossing us around. She commands us to look behind the couch for coins to buy tins of braised beef for dinner. She scrounges up whatever food she can find, from the back of the pantry or from neighbours, fixing breakfasts, lunches and dinners.

When my mother returns days later, grey and shadowy, she comes bearing feasts of doughnuts, hot chicken, bottles of Coke. The deprivation is over, replaced by splendour.

Sometimes she takes us with her. We clamber into the rusty car, taking care not to step on the used syringes on the floor.

I hate and fear the dark, even though I know there is no such thing as monsters, that they're made up like Santa. Each night I tiptoe into my mother's bedroom and slip into bed. If she is not already there, my sister Jacinta comes in too, wriggling into the middle because she is the smallest.

In the mornings, Jacinta and I laugh at my mother's snoring. We jab and prod her. 'Stop snoring, Mummy, you big warthog!'

———

I don't know how to tie my shoes; my mother does them for me.

I don't understand clocks; my mother reads them for me.

I always ask adults to tell me the time. Some try to teach me to read a clock, but I refuse.

My mother bundles us into the car and drives to KFC. I sit in the front seat, to the chagrin of my sisters.

As our car rolls up the drive-through, the speakerbox crackles. 'Welcome to KFC. Can I take your order?'

My mother leans out of the window, glances back at me mischievously, then says, 'BAWK-BAWK.'

'Sorry, I didn't understand that?' comes the voice.

'Bk-bk-BAWK.' I can hear the worker pleading with my mother to stop but she is relentless. 'BAWK BAWK BAWK.'

I giggle so much I think I'm going to die. My mother goes on madly clucking until a gangly teenage boy in a red uniform appears a little way off and starts walking towards our car.

'BAW-shit!' my mother says, and reverses the car out and through a garden, as the teenager watches with his mouth agape. My mother reverses out onto a stretch of road and leans out of the window, throwing out one last 'BAWK!' then puts the pedal to the metal.

When I catch my breath, I ask what we're going to have for dinner now.

'We'll get some McDonald's, darling.' Then she nudges me with her elbow. 'Hey, guess what?'

'What?'

'I should have stayed at KFC. Mummy got scared, though, 'cause she's chicken.'

And I'm laughing again.

Poverty was a part of life, but it was Australian poverty. There was always enough money to chuck two dollars in a chocolate bar skill tester. No matter how poor we were, we could afford to pay money to not win chocolate.

And if we didn't have money, I knew we'd be fine. My mother would just take me shoplifting.

In supermarkets I became an avocado mule, cashew smuggler and strawberry runner. Nobody ever caught me with food stuffed in my underpants. My mother told me I was too clever for them.

One time I shoved a whole box of Coco Pops down my pants and strutted out of the Bi-Lo. It was absurd, and as the automatic doors peeled open, even I thought, *This is ridiculous.*

It was nice to see my mother turn the things I stole into meals. I liked that you didn't need money. You could just take things.

There's a homeless man outside the supermarket, a grimy figure sitting cross-legged in stinging sun. When my mother sees him, she halts to rummage through her leather handbag. She kneels down. 'Give this money to the man,' she says, pressing a two-dollar coin into my hand.

I skip over and pop it in his little hat and he smiles with his blackish mouth.

An explosion reverberates from upstairs and the night flashes an impossible tangerine. For a moment, I think my father's home. He is my theology, my explanation for all things. And my mother and my sisters are screaming like it's him. I stand up, convinced he's here, ready to dash into his tobacco smell, to climb his legs, to feel his moustache graze my cheeks.

Then Rebecca yells, 'The house is on fire!' And we see: smoke surging down the stairs driven by whipping flames.

'Get out, kids!' shouts my mother. 'Fucking get out or we'll be burned alive!'

It doesn't seem as big a deal as she thinks but she grabs my arm and shepherds me out through the sliding glass door as I crane to catch the last glimpse of *Home and Away*. The fire isn't moving so fast; we could have at least waited for the next ad break.

We watch the destruction of our home from the road, see it turn to devastation in the sky.

The fire brigade shows up and turn the hoses on the inferno.

My mother is weeping into the chest of an old woman I've never seen. 'The photos! My jewellery!'

'There, there, dear,' the lady says, patting my mother's back.

A few days later we visit our charred home. We drift through it in silence. Everything is twisted charcoal, like our house has been destroyed and replaced with a black replica. I touch a wall and it crumbles.

I wander upstairs to my room. I imagine what would have happened if I'd been asleep and the fire had trapped me. I decide I would have jumped out of my bedroom window when the smell woke me.

I can hear my mother sobbing and I follow the sound to where she's kneeling in her room, her orange sarong gathering filth in the soot. She's clutching some burnt hoop earrings and shaking her head, her face streaked with mascara.

'Mummy!' sings Jacinta from another room. 'Bunny didn't get burneded!'

Everyone follows Jacinta's voice through the black hallway and we converge in the room where she is standing, in the same pink flower dress she was wearing on the night of the fire, holding her bunny. It's as bright and blue as ever, except for a smear of charred fabric on one of its long ears.

'It's a miracle,' my mother gasps.

'High price for a miracle,' mutters Belinda.

'Shut up,' my mother tells her.

'You dirty little slut!'

I pause the game I'm playing in my room and wander out to the lounge.

Belinda is cowering on the couch as my mother belts her stomach and head with a broom.

'Get out of this fucking house, you slut,' my mother screeches, dragging the word slut out over strikes of the broom.

'Please, Mummy,' sobs Belinda.

My mother keeps going. 'Get out of my house, you filthy slut.'

Belinda rolls off the couch and onto the carpet and curls into a ball.

'Get up,' my mother screams, stabbing at her with the broom, her voice garbled from rum and volume. 'Get out of this house.'

I've never seen my mother this way, like my father.

She drops the broom and leans down and grabs Belinda by the hair, starts dragging her to the door. Belinda screams and stumbles to her feet as my mother opens the screen door then pushes her off the step and onto the front lawn. 'Get out, slut.'

'Mummy!' Belinda screams, running back to get into the house. My mother slams the screen door on her and slams the wooden door too.

'Little slut,' my mother mutters, sitting back down on the couch.

I don't know what Belinda has done but I feel sorry for her. I can see her outside through the window, limping shoeless into the street, her hair tangled.

'Where's Belinda gonna live?' I ask.

'She's a slut, she'll find somewhere.'

My mother has a new boyfriend, Tomsy. He's been in jail for twenty years for raping women but because he's been a good prisoner they've given him parole. He comes to stay with us on weekends.

I like Tomsy, he's funny. One day he puts a pair of my mother's underwear on his head and dances around until everybody runs out of air from laughing.

He's different to my father. He never hits my mother, and when I hit my sisters he sides with them.

Tomsy walks in one day after I've elbowed Belinda in the chest because she's playing my Super Nintendo. 'What's happening here?'

She dobs me in. 'I was just playing and Corey hit me.'

'Corey, come here, mate.'

I know he's going to belt me, but I go anyway. We walk downstairs and sit at the kitchen table. He has never hit me or any of us before and I wonder what he'll do it with.

'You know, I was like you when I was a boy,' he starts, looking at me gently. 'You shouldn't do that to girls. You know it really hurts your mum and sisters. You're a good boy, you don't want to hurt people's feelings, do you?'

'I don't give a shit.'

He reaches over and puts his hand on my shoulder. 'Okay. If you keep hitting people you'll end up in jail. Jail is the scariest place in the world. In jail, people will flog you, all the time.'

'Really?'

'Yeah. People have bashed me a lot. They've nearly killed me.'

'That sounds scary.'

'Every day I wish I never did what I did. I was angry and hurt like you are. I've spent the best years of my life inside a prison cell. I don't want you to waste your life like I have. Do you understand?'

'I think so.'

'How about you go back and say sorry to Belinda? You'll both feel better.'

I jog upstairs to the video game room and sit beside the vast blue beanbag that looks like it's about to swallow Belinda.

'I'm sorry for yelling at you and hitting you, Belinda.'

'Apology accepted,' she says.

I sit then, watching her die over and over in *Super Mario Brothers*, looking at her face each time to see if she'll finally give up.

At last she tosses the controller in my lap. 'I'm done.'

I sit with my mother in our lounge room watching the news of Princess Diana's death.

'She really was the people's princess,' my mother weeps, firing up her bong. 'I reckon it was the Queen behind it,' she says between coughs. 'The Queen's a fucking cunt.'

I'm nine and I still hate school. I rarely go, unless I'm in foster care. At home with my mother, I put up great fights when she brings home a set of encyclopedias, each tome a gorgeous burgundy leather with gold lettering. We've got the whole alphabet, A through Z. Sometimes I take one down from our brown chipboard bookcase, carefully open it to a random page of its tiny writing, and just look at it. I like being around them.

I hassle my mother to let me read encyclopedias instead of going to school.

'Okay,' she caves, 'but you have to read them for an hour every day.'

'Deal,' I say.

One day I open the *S* encyclopedia and browse through it,

marvelling at the words as plentiful as the blades of grass on our lawn.

An article on sin stares up at me from the page, everything my father talks about. It's filled with big words I don't understand. It talks about Christianity, which I do know about. Christianity is about Jesus and forgiveness. From what I can make out, it's saying sin is about mistakes, like a misfired arrow. Good is hitting a target with the arrow.

This idea stays with me for a long time. Sin as mistake. Evil as error.

Rebecca and Belinda never go to foster care. When my mother goes to jail or the Department raids our house, they get to go to Nan's house. I don't know why Nan won't take Jacinta and me. We have a different father to Rebecca and Belinda but we're family too. Nan is our Nan, too.

Foster care is a blur as I spend days and weeks and months waiting to go home. Waiting until I can go back and play video games and drink Coke out of the bottle and live the good life.

I lose or leave behind my Teenage Mutant Ninja Turtle figurines, my favourite blue shorts, my Goosebumps doona. At first I'm upset, but I learn everything is replaceable.

Foster carers don't love me. They don't tell me I'm special or take my head between their hands and machine-gun kisses on my cheeks until I say, 'Ewww,' and pull away. But it's okay because I know I'll always be going back to my mother. She just needs to serve her time in jail or convince the Department to give us back to her.

Cathy Cowan's house is a pigsty. The walls were once white but now they're yellow from Cathy smoking in her chair, on the toilet, in the bath. I see tiny cockroaches in the cutlery draw and I want to vomit.

I eat as little food there as possible. When Cathy serves up watery sausages with gluggy potato mash I can't stop worrying if cockroaches have crawled through it. About the only things I think are clean enough to consume are the lollies Cathy keeps beside her chair. She has been a foster carer for twenty years and, late in the afternoons, when she's had four or five scotch and waters, she boasts of all the foster kids she's looked after.

Ben, her twenty-five-year-old adopted son, still lives with us, and he is going out with Kelly, a fifteen-year-old foster kid, but we can't tell Cathy. She wouldn't understand.

Cathy goes to bed at six each night, right after the news. As soon as she comes out of the shower in a nightie and goes into her bedroom, we play truth or dare. Nobody ever says truth. We always dare each other to kiss or take off our clothes.

Time heals all wounds but the wounds to memory. These wounds it keeps fresh against the years. I grab at a memory I do have and another one, attempting to unite them into a linear narrative. I fail and I have to let them slide back into place, to allow the raw darkness to remain between them.

What happened in these gaps? I know it wasn't something *good* – I didn't find a million dollars in a suitcase or visit the Queen – but the rifts are so vast.

Presumably I have repressed horrific, painful memories. So why do I care that I don't remember? Repression protects. There is safety in blankness. I would do well to drop it. But I want to know the truth about myself.

I wonder if the boy I was knew I was not strong enough to watch from the future that which he suffered directly. Did he hide his desecration to preserve my sanity?

I know these gaps are merciful. But too much was wiped, like when you try to delete a sentence and accidentally eliminate a whole paragraph. I envy others who can remember their childhood. I am episodes, fragments. A second-hand jigsaw puzzle, full of incompleteness.

Am I a liar? No, I'm not a liar. I'm an unreliable narrator.

I *wish* I were a liar. Liars know the truth.

My foster brother Gary is suffocating me with a pillow. I don't know what I've done to make him do this, but I know I'm going to die.

I hold my breath. The sky-blue of the pillowcase becomes blacker and blacker. He is stronger than I am and I'm powerless.

The world reappears and I gulp at it.

'What the fuck are you doing?' yells Ben.

'It's none of your business,' says Gary.

Ben tells him he shouldn't suffocate people, that it's wrong, and I take the opportunity to scamper away.

What would have happened if Ben hadn't stopped Gary suffocating me? Would I have died? I would have died.

Visiting my mother in jail is fun. I feel important when we go through security, being patted down by big stern men in blue uniforms in case we're carrying guns. After, they guide us through concrete hallways.

My mother sits at a wooden table, digging her index finger into her scalp the way she does when she's stressed. Her hair is thinning because of it and she has a small bald patch that makes me embarrassed.

'Mum!' we shout, sprinting for her.

Her eyes light up when she hears and sees us. 'Kids!' she cries, tottering up and towards us. We collide as a family, Rebecca first, then me, Belinda and Jacinta, whirling together in frantic kisses and squeezing hugs.

We sit down for the feast my mother has brought: a block of Cadbury chocolate, a bottle of Coke and a jumbo packet of salt and vinegar chips.

'Eat up,' she says, bouncing Jacinta on her lap, smiling as Belinda digs into the chips. We babble at my mother all afternoon, filling her in on how we're going, complaining about school, relaying everything that's happened in the months since we've seen her.

Our reunion comes to an end when a screw swaggers over.

'Hey, Michelle, gonna have to wrap things up now, get you back to your cell.'

'Yep,' my mother says, chin trembling. She gets to her feet and stretches her arms out like a big bird. 'Okay, kids, come and give Mummy a hug.' We flock to her and bury our heads in her dark green shirt, as she promises to bring us home soon.

I'm sent to live with a foster carer called Jean, a rotund woman with shaved blonde hair. My mother comes to visit while she's on parole to show the Department she can have us children back, and she tells me Jean is a 'lemon', which means she's a lesbian, which I believe is something to do with clits.

I have a big crush on Jean's thirteen-year-old daughter, Elise, who is four years older than me. She is tall, slim, skin gold like my father's, with beautiful shoulder-length brown hair.

One Saturday afternoon, Jean invites friends over for a barbecue. The adults gather around the pool, drinking wine and beer.

Elise fixes herself a cup of water in the kitchen.

'Hey, Elise,' I say, my heart a Morse code machine.

'Yeah?' she says.

I look around to make sure nobody is nearby. The coast is clear, and I gaze into her beautiful green eyes. 'I like you,' I begin. 'I like you a lot.'

'Okay,' she says, leaning against the kitchen bench.

A numbing terror. 'When I see you my doodle gets big.'

Her eyes shoot up. 'Oh, wow. Why don't you show me?' Before I can answer, she takes my hand and pulls me into the bathroom.

I pull my boardshorts down a little to show her my erect doodle.

'Wow,' she murmurs. She leans forward to kiss me on my lips, her tongue winding wetly into my mouth. 'Come with me,' she says.

She leads me out of the bathroom, through the house and into my bedroom. She shuts the doors behind us and walks a few metres in front of me.

'Are you ready?' she asks.

'Yes.'

She turns her back to me. I wait, my stomach feeling the way a trampoline does when an adult steps on it. Stretchy, heavy.

It happens in slow motion: her hands reach behind her, grip the edges of her fluoro-orange one-piece swimsuit and pull it inwards, upwards, into a wedgie. I stare agog at her butt cheeks and am overcome with panic. Her arse is so scary and big and, even though I feel my doodle strain against my boardshorts, I don't want to do this any more. I run out of the room, slamming the door shut behind me, racing through the house, down the stairs. I bomb dive into the pool and stay under the water for as long as I can.

My cheeks are molten with shame. I should have fucked her. Why couldn't I fuck her? My father would have fucked her.

I hate all my foster carers with one exception: Tim and Leslie.

Sometimes when foster carers need a break from you, they send you to respite carers. Tim and Leslie are respite carers, which means I can't stay with them for very long. I spend weekends there, from Friday night until Sunday afternoon.

They're in their forties. Leslie is milky-white, with short grey hair. Tim is tall and handsome.

'Hello, Corey,' they say opening the front door the first time I go to stay with them, smiling broadly. 'Welcome to our home.'

Suddenly, I see a furry golden rocket scrabbling over the white tiles towards me, their pet dog.

'Charlie, let Corey get in the door first,' Tim says sternly as Charlie winds through Leslie's legs and leaps at me.

He's gorgeous and I drop to my knees and run my fingers through his soft fur as he licks my face with his squishy wet tongue.

'Would you like to see your room?' Leslie asks in a voice I've decided I like the sound of.

'Yes, please.'

Their house is so nice and clean.

When I walk through their door, when I sit down to dinner at their beautiful wooden dinner table, when I float on my back in their pool for hours in the sun, when I go to sleep curled up with Charlie, I feel warm and cosy.

Charlie the golden retriever is running around the edge of the pool, yipping.

'Leslie,' I sing out from my bed of pool noodles. 'Can Charlie swim with me?'

She looks up from her newspaper. Her big black sunglasses and long white legs make her look like a frog. 'He really shouldn't be in the pool.'

'But he really wants to hop in!' I press on, sensing a victory.

As if to make his case, Charlie begins whining, training his big brown puppy dog eyes on Leslie.

'Pretty please,' I say to Leslie.

'Ohhh-kay,' she says. 'Charlie, you can go in.' She clicks her fingers in the direction of the pool and Charlie is already airborne. He bellyflops into the water inches from my head and I giggle as he doggy paddles over to me.

I throw the tennis ball for Charlie and he motors towards it, snapping at it clumsily, barking at his own incompetence. We play like this for hours, until the sun is going down.

At night, we watch Disney movies together in the lounge room, sharing a block of chocolate. Tim and Leslie keep a nightlight on in my room so there is no darkness and I fall asleep with Charlie lying beside me.

When I'm there, I want to be the best I can be for them. Tim and Leslie and Charlie are better than my family. I wish I was their son.

One night after dinner, Tim and Leslie bring out dessert and then they go quiet.

'Corey,' Tim says, a solemn look on his face, reaching out and clasping Leslie's hand. 'We have to talk to you about something.'

I watch their faces, waiting for bad news.

'Would you like it if we adopted you? Would you like to be our son?'

'Yes,' I say, my stomach soaring like a kite.

———

I race home from school on a Friday ready to go to Tim and Leslie's house.

Jean is sitting on the couch watching TV.

'You're not going to Tim and Leslie's house this weekend.'

'Why not?'

'They can't take you any more.'

I go to my room and sit down on my bed in shock. I can feel myself getting ready to cry but I don't let the tears out.

They were lying about wanting me.

A social worker arrives a little later to take me to a new respite home. I ask her why Tim and Leslie won't take me any more.

'Leslie is sick so she has to get better. They say they're sorry.'

I look at the social worker in the eye, with her clean black pants and her nice white collared shirt, her neatly brushed blonde hair and bright blue eyes. 'Tell them they're cunts and I hate them. I'll kill them if I ever see them again.'

I'm on top of Rhys Christiansen, in the playground mulch, and I'm choking him. Girls are screaming around me but I go on throttling him. I summon every bit of power in my body and force it through my fingers.

He's dying. I can tell because his punches come more slowly, like they're moving through jelly.

A teacher tears me off him and he gasps for air.

In the principal's office they ask me why I did it.

'I didn't like his freckles.'

It's true. We'd been playing soccer in the playground, on the same team, and the ball had been kicked away and he'd started to jog to it and I'd looked at him and a rage had overcome me. I stuck my leg out and tripped him.

'What'd you do that for?' he'd whined from the ground, and then I was on top of him.

I stare down the principal, feeling powerful because I'm a psycho to him. I like that people will be scared of me. I feel invincible, like how in *Super Mario Brothers* Mario touches a star and nothing can hurt him. I am bad, and I like being bad. I throw desks at teachers, I hit kids with chairs.

I know eight-year-old boys aren't supposed to be like this, but I am not like other boys. I am different, special. I am my father's son, and they will fear me.

My social worker picks me up from school to visit a potential placement.

A woman answers the screen door. 'Hi,' she says cheerily through the mesh of maroon metal. When it swings open, I look at her. She's slim with blonde hair, and wearing light blue denim jeans and a white blouse.

'I'm Tracey.'

Standing behind her are three kids, the biological children. We say hello and then they go to their rooms.

I sit down at the kitchen table and ask Tracey what it's like living with her.

'What is this, Twenty Questions?' she jokes.

I keep peppering her with questions.

'Are you allowed to watch *The Simpsons* here?' I ask. One foster carer prohibited it because Bart Simpson is 'a corrupting influence'.

Tracey chuckles. 'The kids love watching *The Simpsons*. I don't think it's very funny, quite juvenile really, but they're allowed to watch it.'

I continue my interrogation. 'What about pocket money?'

Tracey looks at the social worker and then back at me. 'You're a curious little fella, aren't you?'

I remain impassive, waiting for her answer. If I have to go to a new foster home, I want it to be a good one.

'All the kids get five dollars a week, and they can earn more if they do chores.'

'Wow.' I am impressed. 'What about Milo?'

'What do you mean, what about Milo?' Tracey asks.

'Do you drink Milo here?'

'No, we don't drink Milo because it's too expensive.' She fetches a cigarette from her packet and lights it.

'I don't like smoking,' I say, waving the smoke away from my face, which isn't quite true. I like when my parents smoke. But they roll their own and it smells different.

Tracey gives a pinched smile. 'Well, it's *my* house so I'm allowed to smoke. When you get your own house, feel free to ban smoking.'

Something about the way she says it, the annoyance in her voice, bothers me, and I decide I don't want to live here.

As we get in the car to leave, the social worker asks what I thought of Tracey.

I don't like her. There's something not quite right about her. Something about the lines around her mouth. Her eyes are too piercingly blue. Her blonde, wavy hair is too nicely brushed. And she was suspiciously nice. I can tell when people are pretending. Social workers faked being nice because it was their job and they didn't want to upset you. My mother faked being nice like that when the Department sent people to inspect our house. Tracey was being fake nice because she wanted me so she'd get money for me. I did the same thing, to trick people, when I wanted something.

'I don't want to live there,' I tell the social worker, as Tracey and her three kids wave goodbye to us in the front yard.

'Okay,' she says, backing the car out onto the street. 'We'll keep looking at places for you.'

A few days later, I'm watching television in the lounge room when a gleaming Department car appears in the driveway. The social worker climbs out and comes inside to tell me I'm moving in with Tracey tonight.

I'm stunned. I said I didn't want to live with Tracey. I thought the Department had to do what kids wanted.

'Corey,' the social worker says firmly, 'you have nowhere else to go.'

I stop arguing. She's telling the truth.

3

'Your mother passed away last night,' says the social worker with bureaucratic compassion.

We sit at the kitchen table and Tracey places her arm around my shoulder too readily, an artificial gesture. I have this sudden strange sensation that I'm on a candid camera show and, any moment now, a grinning host will leap out and reveal the trick, my mother cackling behind him.

'It's going to be okay,' continues the social worker in a tone that suggests she cares deeply, which is a lie. I am a 'case' to her, one number among many. I want to howl down the heartlessness of her sympathy, but I feel a lump in my throat I know will disintegrate if I open my mouth. So I stay silent until it passes, then I wipe my eyes, drink down the remaining brine in my throat and ask what's going to happen to me now.

'You'll stay in care until you're eighteen,' the social worker says. 'Tracey has agreed to let you stay with her.'

Tracey nods at the social worker, smiles reassuringly at me and rubs my back. 'You're part of our family now.'

I stumble, dazed, to my room and lie down in bed. A few minutes later, Tracey comes in to sit beside me. I curl into her warmth, close my eyes and let the hot sea win.

I am alone now. I will stay in foster care forever.

More than two decades after her death and my mother is only a spectre in a half-remembered dream. She has assumed the nature of a myth. So many of my memories of how she looked are memories only of the photographs I have seen of her. How did her perfume smell? Did she hug soft or hard?

Michelle Mary Butler: my mother, my abstraction. She was real once. Now she is only qualities, a Cubist painting. Now she is components, fractured and sterile. I can see her thick black eyelashes but not her eyes, can see the cracked soles of her feet but not the shape of her toes.

I remember her possessions more vividly. The objects which she used to make herself feel beautiful: a pair of elegant light-brown sandals, silver peacock earrings, a garish teal hairbrush, a sarong originally a royal purple until the years washed its brilliance away.

If I arrange these objects in my mind, the emptiness between them is my mother.

I wish my memory were more powerful. I wish I had a memory of her face in sunshine, that I could recall her visage just by closing my eyes.

I have asked my sisters and other people about my mother but they describe her with adjectives. Useless things that communicate nothing. When somebody says she was warm, it leaves me cold. When they tell me she loved me, it's just sterile information. Mars is the fourth planet from the sun, Moscow is the capital of Russia, and my mother loved me.

I examine the bare facts of who she was. She was a drug addict who left her children alone for days. How might I be different if I'd grown up with a mother? Perhaps if she had lived, I would have grown up to hate her?

I don't know.

There is in me a canyon of shame. That I called my mother a slut, that I didn't try to stop my father beating her, that I hit her myself. It must have hurt her. I wish I had another chance to be her son.

I have an enduring fantasy that one day I'll receive a letter from her. In it, she'll tell me she was forced to go into witness protection after informing on drug dealers, that it was decided for her safety it was necessary to pretend she had died. 'My beautiful baby boy,' she will write in the sloping cursive I vaguely remember from the letters she sent from prison. 'I am so sorry I've been away all these years and missed out on so much. The drug dealers who were after me have died and the police tell me I'm free to resume my old life.'

I go months without thinking of her but when I do she is all I can think about. I rack my brain, hunting for details, stories, conversations, the ones which haven't been ravaged by time and substances. There are so few.

———

Her funeral is a week later. I sit with my sisters in the pews of a spartan chapel and watch everybody crying around me. All three of my sisters cling to each other, blubbering 'Mummy' over and over. I don't cry, which bothers me. You are supposed to cry at your mother's funeral. To hide my tearlessness, I stare down at my shoes during the long service.

Our mother is being cremated. I keep hoping she isn't dead, that halfway through I'll hear one of her animal screams, they'll expunge some hidden fire, and then she will be back with a melted grin.

To the tune of Celine Dion's 'My Heart Will Go On', we shuffle out of the chapel to deposit her ashes into a wall, into a green box set in cream bricks. I stand beside my sisters and my nan to receive the funeral attendees.

'Corey.' I look up to see the social worker who brought me to the funeral. 'We have to go now, I'm sorry.'

Tracey has organised a holiday to Victoria. She has already driven down with her children and she expects me to join them.

'I don't want to go.'

'You can't miss your plane.'

'I don't want to go on a fucking plane, on a fucking holiday! Why can't I just stay here?'

The social worker smiles awkwardly. 'This is just what we have to do.'

Before the funeral, before she'd left for Victoria, I'd argued with Tracey about wanting to stay with my family, just for a little while, but she'd insisted. 'You're a part of *this* family now.'

I'd told her to go fuck herself. 'You're just a foster mother, doing this for money!'

'Right, that's twenty minutes in the corner,' she'd said.

I stormed into the laundry and sat down. Tracey stomped into the kitchen, leaned over the stove and set the timer, which would buzz when I'd done my time.

'Don't think just because your mum died that you can get away with being a brat,' she said.

I elbowed the washing machine behind me as I stared her down, hurting myself but not betraying the pain.

'Make that thirty minutes,' Tracey said, readjusting the timer.

I turn to my sisters and Nan. 'I have to go on this stupid holiday.'

Nan looks embarrassed by my outburst and I pull away as she offers me a hug. *She could have stopped this – she could have taken me in.* I embrace my sisters quickly then slouch back with the social worker to the Department car.

Years later, a memory, a thunderbolt. A few days before my mother's death, she had phoned to speak with me but I refused to take the call because I was busy playing video games. Had my callousness driven my mother into one last heroin-fuelled blowout? It's entirely possible.

———

A review of my placement with Tracey is held a few months later. I take the day off school and we drive to the Department's offices, walk inside the air-conditioned building that towers above the flat business district around it, ascend through its belly in a stainless-steel elevator.

'How's it going with Tracey, Corey?' asks a woman with a double chin and cheeks riddled with rosacea.

'I don't want to live with her,' I say.

'Why?' asks another social worker.

'Because she's shit. She's a bad person.'

'Corey,' Tracey coos beside me, smiling beatifically the way she always does when I publicly disobey her. Her voice grows higher, more feminine, less menacing – I think of this in my mind in capitals, as The Voice.

When the meeting ends we walk silently out of the building, the Department convinced I am just trouble.

As the maroon van hurtles down the highway, Tracey scowls at me through the rear-view mirror. 'Don't ever pull that rot again. And you're grounded for a month.'

After that, I had very little to do with the Department while I was living with Tracey. It appeared to them that I was in a stable, caring placement.

On the odd occasion a social worker did come to the house to inspect it and ask me how things were going, Tracey wove my anger in her favour.

One afternoon, as I sat in the kitchen waiting for a social worker to arrive, I told Tracey that I'd be telling them about everything that was happening. 'They're gonna take me away from you to somewhere better.'

She smirked. 'You don't get it, do you? There's nowhere else for you to go, Corey. Who would take you?'

My abiding memory of those years with Tracey is hunger.

Her promise of pocket money evaporated with the arrival of Sarah and Mikayla, two more foster kids, sisters, who arrived a few months after me. Mikayla was thirteen, pallid and gangly, with frizzy red hair that lent her the appearance of constant electrocution. Sarah, on the other hand, was pretty, a year older than me, with strawberry-blonde hair, blue eyes and a light tan.

From then on, there was never enough food in the house, with six kids all packing school lunches. Most days, I took two rice cakes with Vegemite smeared between them and, if I was lucky, an orange.

Puberty had begun to make me grow and I was always ravenous, wolfing down my dinner, virtually inhaling it.

'Don't be greedy,' Tracey would snipe from across the kitchen table.

I couldn't help it; I was so hungry. I regularly offered to wash the dishes just so I could scrape food remnants off the fry pan. Hunger became a constant dull throb in my head.

It wasn't as though Tracey was strapped for cash. She was a chain smoker and drank bottles of ginger wine each night. She could afford to buy country music albums, the odd guitar here and there. She just didn't seem to care. 'There's not enough food,' we'd tell her, and she'd say we were too lazy to find any.

This wasn't true, though. We each hustled in our own way. Mikayla and Sarah were caught on several occasions pilfering from Tracey's purse. I stumbled on the idea of earning extra cash for food by hunting down kids at school with money and offering a unique business opportunity.

'Hey,' I'd say, flashing my winningest smile. 'Need someone to go get you food from the tuckshop?' I charged twenty cents a delivery and promised to push in line if need be so they'd receive their goodies quickly and could properly enjoy their lunch break.

Business boomed. Each day I'd spend the first twenty minutes of lunch racing madly around cradling cans of Coke, sausage rolls, chips and lollies. Then I'd return to the tuckshop with my loot, usually around three or four dollars. Finally, I'd kick back and savour the rewards of my labour, a steaming-hot sausage roll drizzled in a combination of barbecue and tomato sauce, feeling like a kid Bill Gates.

About a month into the venture, though, disaster struck. A kid named Dean, also poor if his grimy face was anything to go by, cottoned on and began to compete with me. I knew something was up when I saw him lurching past the school office, a stack of meat pies nestled in his arms and a can of lemonade under his chin. There was absolutely no way he could have afforded that bounty.

The situation turned out to be even worse than I initially thought. Dean was only charging ten cents a delivery. In one fell swoop, this buck-toothed, piss-smelling dunderhead, this *idiot*, had destroyed my business. Customers flocked to him.

In hindsight, with the benefit of a superficial knowledge of economics, I should have approached him and suggested colluding to keep prices high. We could have had a poor-kid cartel. What I did instead was drop my price to ten cents too, but after one lunch time of pestering people who'd already been served by Dean left me with the paltry sum of sixty cents, I never delivered – or ate – sausage rolls again.

Tracey enforced bizarre, severe punishments. If you swore or misbehaved, she'd send you to sit in the corner for hours. Once, I sat in the corner from 10 in the morning until 8 at night. The trick was to try to make myself disappear in my head. To pretend I was a wall or the wind.

Another time I threw a temper tantrum and she banned me from using electricity for a week in the middle of a steamy Queensland summer. Or she might hop onto my computer and uninstall a game I'd been playing, which led to strange situations where she'd bark, 'How do I uninstall this game? Where do I click?' I'd guide her through the uninstall process.

It was so absurdly specific to me I can't help but laugh.

I hate when Tracey tickles me. I hate being touched, especially by her. She doesn't tickle me like my mother did. She doesn't do it gently. She jabs hard, like a machine.

It comes out of nowhere, when she is in one of her rare tipsy moods.

She sits on me and I think she's going to bust my ribs.

'Fuck off, Tracey,' I laugh.

'Don't swear.'

'Fuck off!' I giggle.

'Right,' she declares, getting up off me. 'That's twenty minutes in the corner.'

'But you were tickling me,' I protest.

'Go,' she commands, and I do.

These events aren't in the past, for me. I still think about them most days, I dream about them. There is no such thing as the past. Linearity is a myth, memory a time machine, trauma an acid eating the wiring, consuming the machine. It malfunctions.

Tracey has three biological children, Nick, Kylie, and Matt, who I share a bedroom with. I'd always wanted a bigger brother and he is how I imagine a big brother should be. He dominates me, but he is ready to protect me, with violence if necessary. A boy from the neighbourhood pushes me during a game of backyard cricket and Matt grabs him by his collar and tells him if he ever does that again, he'll be dead meat.

Matt is a couple of years older than me, mid-puberty, but we quickly become close. We gang up on the girls, cupcaking them with our farts, dressing in their clothes and pretending to be the stupid Spice Girls. He is taller than me, tanned and teenage-volatile. He has shoulders speckled with ugly red pimples and a massive Adam's apple that reminds me of the snake in *Anaconda* after it eats Jon Voight.

What I like best about Matt is how we form alliances. On Wednesday nights, Tracey bundles us up and we drive a few suburbs away to attend a country music night. While the adults sit around drinking, talking and playing guitar, the kids play touch football. Matt and I refuse to play against each other. We insist on being on the same team because we're brothers. Our pairing is inarguable. It is always Matt and me against the rest, and we defeat everyone easily.

Matt and I kill cane toads together too. He shows me new methods including pushing the lawnmower over them, the goriest way of all, which we quickly reject because it leaves our legs covered with mince.

'What are you doing?' I ask him one sweating indigo night. He's hunched over a cane toad he has pressed into the earth with a cricket stump, holding a white cylinder of Saxa salt over the creature, like a necromancer performing some ritual of death.

'Salt.'

'Salt?'

'Salt.'

I watch him tip the salt onto the toad's leathery brown back. A few seconds pass. I wait for some spectacular death. Maybe it will explode, or start frothing from its mouth. Nothing happens. The cane toad just squirms uncomfortably.

'It's not dying,' I say, disappointed.

Matt lifts the cricket stump from the toad and lets it hop away. 'Don't worry, it'll die later.'

———

I'm woken up by someone hopping into my bed with me. I rub my eyes and see Matt leaning in close to me. 'What are you doing?' I ask.

'Shhhhh.' He bends forward and I feel his tongue burst into my mouth like a squid. At the same time, he grabs my hand and forces it down his pants and onto his penis. Then he moves my hand so it holds his dick, moves it up and down. Soon he groans and hot goo spills over and through my fingers.

He gets up and returns to his bed. Within minutes he is snoring while I lie in the dark feeling odd.

At breakfast the next morning, Matt calls me gay for putting honey on my Weet-Bix.

'Stuff you, Matt! *You're* gay.'

He looks at me like he's going to kill me so I shut my trap.

It continues. By day he is my big brother and in the nights he invades my body. I don't think to fight back as it progresses. He shoves his dick into my mouth and fucks my head until he sighs and I can taste the salty goo and have to go to the toilet to spit it out.

He acquires a bottle of baby oil and fucks me. It hurts but it's over quickly. I just lie there on my belly and let him do it until he gets up.

We go on a camping holiday and originally he's going to sleep in a tent with Nick, but then he insists on sleeping in my tent.

'You promise you and Corey won't annoy the girls?' Tracey asks.

'I promise, Mum,' he tells her.

He's never violent but the next day I have difficulty walking.

I don't know if Tracey had any inkling of what Matt was doing.

———

A few years ago, I was talking with audience members in the bar after a show.

I spotted a red, lumpy woman bobbing nervously. Her face seemed familiar. A name popped into my head. 'Georgia?'

'Yes,' she smiled. 'That's me. Do you remember me?'

'You worked for the Department, right?'

'Yep.'

Without thinking, I blurt out, 'Did you know about Tracey and Matt?'

She nodded, with regret I thought.

Somebody tapped me on the shoulder and I looked away briefly.

I turned back to talk to Georgia again and she was gone.

Each Christmas, the state foster carers' organisation held an annual Christmas party for foster families. Foster children from all over south-east Queensland would descend upon a massive conference centre ringed with lawns. Tinsel hung from gnarled eucalyptus trees and towering palms. An ocean of tables brimmed with ham and cheese and turkey and prawns and crackling and lollies and fairy bread. It was paradise.

For some reason, local bikie gangs would attend every year too. They'd give the children rides on their motorcycles, roaring through the streets as we screamed with joy in the sidecars or clung for dear life to the backs of these grizzled outsider angels, feeling the fat leather-vested torsos, warm from the sun. They were all old, hard men with massive grey beards; every one looked like an S&M version of

Santa, all leather and chains. Tearing through the streets on their loud, growling steeds you felt like you mattered, that you weren't just another kid wearing second-hand school uniforms and missing out on school camps because they were too expensive. After we rode with the bikies on their motorcycles we'd go back to the park and open presents they had bought for us. Good presents, too, tailored for each individual child.

I looked at the bikies and wished I was one of their children. I imagined the wonderful times the children of bikies have, I pictured them being tucked in at night.

While Tracey's own children swan about, living the high life, the foster children have entered a bizarre arms race of grovelling.

'Tracey,' Sarah says, in her sweetest voice, 'may I go to my friend Erin's house on Thursday to practise for our dance at school assembly?'

'Don't suck up to me, Sarah.'

'I'm not!' Sarah says, pitch rising girlishly, a show of brittleness, like a dog extending its head in a pose of vulnerability that says 'I'm no threat'.

'You *are* sucking up,' Mikayla chimes in, betraying her own sister, despite having been on Tracey's bad side herself only hours earlier. It is ghoulish, cartoonish. But to ally with Tracey now will, hopefully, buy her a state of grace for a little while.

———

Navigating life in the house with Tracey was so labyrinthine, so fraught, not even Alan Turing could have done it. He would have spent hours in the corner looking at the intersection of two walls, grounded for eating a packet of noodles. Over time, the part of me that resisted the nonsense of it, the natural recognition of injustice, became quieter and quieter until it was silenced. A helplessness set in, a fatalism grew. We basically lived with a cyclone. There could be no engagement with it, just acceptance of its inevitability.

The foster children had second-hand uniforms, shitty shoes. When Kylie went to high school in a brand-new school uniform, Tracey lied and said, 'The school didn't have any second-hand uniforms.'

I showed up on the first day of high school in a uniform that was visibly second-hand, which added to my growing sense of being dirty and poor. It was a feeling similar to the one I had when I was young, of being exceptional – only the opposite. *There's something wrong with me.* My high school's uniform was olive green with gold trim. That's how it was supposed to look. Mine, on the other hand, was worn and tired. The golden school logo on my shirt had all but disappeared and now looked as if I had dropped egg on myself. When I answered questions in class, I made sure to angle my arm in such a way as to not reveal the holes in the pit of my shirt.

———

I am disgusting. She tells me all the time. When I eat my food too quickly at dinner, I'm disgusting. When I come home sweaty from playing cricket, I'm disgusting.

Tracey takes me to buy shoes for the first time in three years. My old pair hurt my toes and each shoe has a huge hole in its sole, a gap replicated in every one of my four pairs of socks. It has been raining and water has saturated my shoes, socks and feet. Every step I take comes with a squelching sound and my feet are wrinkled as if I've stayed in a bath too long. When I take my shoes off to try on new ones, my feet reek. Tracey's face mutates above me. 'Ugh, you disgusting pig. You dirty boy.'

I feel ashamed. I know my feet stink and that I am disgusting, but I cannot help it. I have no other shoes to wear – I have been begging her for months for new ones. I look to the teenage shop assistant kneeling in front of me and am filled with gratitude that he doesn't call me disgusting too.

In Year 8, I make friends with Trent, a kid who lives a few streets over, and who I use for the food his mother provides. I know he has no other friends, that he's desperate. His mother is relieved someone wants to play with her manic, goofy son and plies me with sausage rolls and Coke. It's a sweet situation for me.

I race over to Trent's house every afternoon to gorge on food and play cricket in his backyard because he has a net. One summer holidays I bat for two whole days straight, amassing a score of 897 before Trent quits. His face is massively sunburnt. Meanwhile, I'm trying to make 1000 runs. A perverse part of me enjoys seeing this kid who I think is rich be broken by me, a filthy foster kid.

In the late afternoon air, he finally manages to dismiss me, clean bowls me. I drop the bat and go to walk home.

'It's your turn to bowl to me!'

'Gotta go home, sorry,' I laugh like a shithead.

'That's unfair!' I hear him protesting from behind me. 'I've bowled to you for days!'

I jog to the gate, chuckling darkly to myself.

Suddenly there is an explosion in the back of my head and my vision flashes black. I fall to the ground, pain shooting through my body.

Trent appears upside-down above me. 'I'm so sorry. Are you okay?'

The world seems dimmer and black spots swim through it, like particles in a science textbook's illustration of Brownian motion. 'What happened?'

'I threw the cricket ball and it accidentally hit you in the back of the head.'

'Fuck you!' I shout, getting up to my feet. 'Why the fuck would you do that? I could have died.' I shove him, his gut wobbling as he stumbles back.

'I'm sorry,' Trent says, his milky face crumpling.

'You're a fuckhead,' I shout, jumping the fence and heading home.

When I get back to Tracey's house, she is waiting at the front door.

'Trent's mother just called me,' she says, blocking my entrance. 'She said you called him a fuckhead.'

'Yeah, I did. He pelted a cricket ball into the back of my head when I was walking away.'

'You're going to go back there and apologise.'

'What?' I say in disbelief.

'You're going back to apologise to Trent and his mother. You will not undermine my reputation in this neighbourhood.'

'I've been hit in the back of the head with a cricket ball. I need to go to a doctor!'

'Oh, you're fine, don't be such a wuss. You're grounded for two weeks – go back and apologise now or it'll be a month.'

I head back to Trent's house, certain I am going to collapse and die of a brain haemorrhage.

His mother answers the door. 'Hello, Corey.'

'Hi, Mrs Nichols. Tracey said I had to apologise for before.'

She looks at me quizzically. 'Okay? Well, Trent would actually like to say sorry to you.' Craning her neck upwards she calls for him.

He thunders down the stairs, sees me and says, 'I'm so sorry, man. I'm an idiot.'

'I'm sorry too,' I say in appeasement, remembering that I needed to come over here for food in the future. 'I shouldn't have yelled at you.' I tell him I have to get home now because Tracey has grounded me.

I fantasised about playing cricket for Australia. On weekends, I played imaginary cricket with myself, setting up a bin in the backyard to bowl against and playing out entire test matches. I wished I could play for a club against real people. I asked Tracey if I could join one but she said it wasn't possible because I was too angry. Her answer made me angry, but I didn't show it, realising I'd only prove her point. And she was right. I was my father's son. There was something scary and red inside me.

Whenever I was sent to the kitchen corner, slumped on the sticky linoleum, I could feel anger like acid eating away at my arteries, melting my veins, scarring my organs. I wished I could shoot all the anger out of my eyes and destroy her.

But I couldn't. I wasn't a superhero. I had no special powers. I had no power at all.

I vowed to myself that one day Tracey would pay for this. One day I would kill her. Years from now, when I was a man, I'd come for her in the night, when she least expected it.

These thoughts of revenge were a salve for my anger, made it so I didn't feel as if my fury would send my heart rocketing out of my chest. The hours in the corner dissolved in homicidal reverie. It calmed me, imagining with expansive glee all the things I would do to her, the way I would slice her flesh away, cut, burn and stomp her. I'd piss and shit on her, fill her with knives and brooms, do everything to her that my father had done to my mother and worse, far worse.

Eventually I'd come back to reality when she told me I could leave the corner. I'd stand up, feet numb, almost disappointed to be leaving my sanctuary. I'd smile at her, revel in her ignorance of my plans, my secret hate, which was so much larger and final than her. She had no idea what was coming. I was evil. I was invincible. She couldn't take that from me.

———

Tracey became worse over time. Unchecked by social services, unresisted by any of us, her cruelty metastasised.

When I was thirteen, an intellectually impaired toddler named Teddy came to stay with us. He had a joyous spirit and was overwhelmingly cute. We were all very fond of him, and the girls fought among themselves to fuss over him.

One night in bed, I heard a commotion and opened my bedroom door to investigate. Tracey had Teddy up on the laundry basin.

'You disgusting little boy,' she snarled. He cried a big wet mewl and shivered. 'Filthy, filthy!' Tracey hissed, dropping his shitty nappy in the laundry basin.

I saw her slap him, heard the dull thwack of her hand on his misshapen head. He pulled away in pain and she slapped him on the cheek then again on top of the head. 'Filthy.'

I felt a surge of anger. 'What the fuck are you doing, Tracey?'

Tracey spun around. 'Get to bed now, Corey.'

'Don't hit Teddy.'

'I didn't hit him.'

'I *saw* you hit him.'

'Stop your lying! Get to bed now!' she said, her voice a sharpness I feared.

Just like that my bravery crumbled. 'I'm sorry,' I said, retreating into my room.

In bed, I kicked myself for speaking out. Would she punish me for my insolence? What had I been thinking, standing up for Teddy?

It was illegal for foster carers to hit children. What if Tracey thought I'd tell the Department? What if she killed me so I wouldn't tell the Department about what I saw?

I told myself I was being silly. There was no way Tracey would kill me. She wouldn't be able to explain it.

While I withdrew into myself, Matt got angrier, more defiant, until one day he came close to punching Tracey. He pinned her against a wall and she grabbed him by the ear and dragged him down to the ground. I caught a glimpse of it by accident as I walked out of the toilet. I wasn't sure whose team I was on. Torturer or rapist.

In the aftermath, he was sent to live with his father thousands of kilometres away.

There was a knock on my bedroom door.

'Come in,' I said, pausing *Age of Empires*.

It was Tracey. 'Hey, Core,' she said in The Voice. 'I've got a question for you. Can I come in?'

Something was up. She wanted something. 'Of course, Tracey.'

She sat down on my bed carefully. 'The Department has asked . . .' She trailed off girlishly. 'If you want to give a speech about how good being in foster care has been for you. I think it'll be good for you to do.' She scrunched her face up in a friendly way. 'Plus you'll get the day off school.'

I knew what this meant: if I spoke about how good foster care was, it would reflect well on her, which in turn would help me.

I agreed to do it.

'Great! It's next week. On the way home we can get some Macca's too.' She stood up and looked at me. 'You're such a smart boy, Corey.'

I wrote and performed the speech at a foster care event, and then it was printed in an internal foster carer newsletter.

Cameron's Story

Hello, my name is 'Cameron' (not my real name) and I am a foster child and I have been in foster care for a good part of my life. I would like to explain to all present what it is like being a foster child and to voice my opinion of foster care.

When I first came into foster care I felt scared and a little confused as to why I was suddenly living with these people. I also felt anger towards Family Services for separating me from my family. I realise now that I was a very angry and confused boy and I would have been a tough placement for any foster carer. I am therefore grateful for those foster carers who took me on when I was considered a child with behavioural problems.

For a few years I drifted in and out of different placements. This only served to fuel my resentment for Family Services, but I now know that Family Services were doing what was right for me in the long run.

Some of the foster carers that I was placed with were great, some were flexible and some were very safety-conscious. All these foster carers had some form of good attributes. I think that a well-rounded foster carer is someone who has all these attributes.

There is one attribute that I believe all foster carers should excel in and that is to encourage a fair and friendly environment. For instance, it is much easier to get along with a foster carer who is friendly and who you know will listen to your side of the story (or argument), than it is to get along with a foster carer who keeps themselves at a distance from you. It is also important that a foster carer be a little flexible but come down on the child when they have to. What I mean by this is the foster child has just come from a completely different house and has to suddenly adjust to the new carer's rules and so the foster carer needs to show flexibility. If the foster carer shows flexibility it shows that they are trying to help.

With some of my foster carers it felt like they gave their own children more respect than they gave us foster kids. I can understand that they feel an itsy-bitsy bit closer to their own child than their foster kids. In some of my experiences it didn't seem like the foster parents went to any great length to conceal it.

One of the most annoying things I hate, and still do, is pity. As a foster child I don't need pity. I need support and I am sure a great number of foster kids out there would agree with me. A lot of foster kids come from homes where rape, abuse and drugs are a part and parcel of everyday life. Do you think they are going to need pity? No, they are going to need support. So it is therefore the foster carer's duty to support the foster child in every aspect of his or her life.

There is one really good thing that has come out of foster care for me and that is a stable home environment. Tonnes of foster carers go out of their way to promote a very stable home environment which is a big plus for foster kids. On the other hand some of the parents of foster children mightn't ever be home, and they let the kid or kids smoke, drink or take drugs.

The foster care system has enabled me to have stability and security in a safe, loving environment and I am grateful for having had the chance to experience these things.

Now I will conclude my speech with a big thank you to Family Services and the hardworking foster carers.

I recognise myself in the boy who wrote that, particularly when he asserts that 'all these foster carers had some form of good attributes'. I see the dogged insistence on the ultimate goodness of people. Yet at the same time there's an alien quality to his words. They have the glossy vagueness of propaganda. I hated writing them but I did it out of fear of what Tracey would do to me if I didn't. The most telling thing is that nowhere in the speech do I ever thank Tracey. It is a tiny rebellion hidden in a larger act of appeasement.

A sneering face, its top lip curled in disgust. That's how I remember Tracey in my nightmares. It's a look that says *you're pathetic* with the undeniable force of a prophecy. It's a mask of contempt, napalm making you into specks. The gaze of Medusa, which she trained on me so many times, on all of us.

Once Mikayla rode a new bike Kylie was given for her birthday. It was a nice bike, a gleaming gold frame with a canary-yellow seat. In what must have been the worst thing that could happen to a teenage girl, Mikayla ended up getting period blood on the seat.

When Kylie saw it she screamed in outrage. Tracey marched down from the computer room where she spent most of her time in internet chat rooms. When she saw the crimson smear across the yellow bike seat she lost her mind.

'You disgusting pig, Mikayla. You dirty, dirty grub,' Tracey sneered.

These incidents were commonplace and I spent a lot of time thinking about how to avoid Tracey's punishments. I decided in the end that being as nice as possible was the best strategy. I couldn't fight back or flee so instead I fawned. I sided with her against myself. I betrayed myself to appease her.

After years of this, I forgot what I was trying to protect. The only voice left in my head was hers, the voice I imitated in the terrible bargain I'd struck. I disappeared. She reigned, outside and inside me.

Tracey didn't like it when we got angry. The best way to placate her was to be nice. Tracey didn't want to see my anger, my fragility.

I'd weed the garden in order to curry favour with her, hoping it would buy me some kind of goodwill for when she snapped. It never worked. I could spend all day bent over, ripping my hands up, and she'd still turn on me for not hearing her yelling out from her computer room while I was in the backyard. I could wash dishes apropos of nothing and I was just as liable to be sent to the corner for not saying thank you loud enough after dinner.

As a kid, I didn't clue on to the fact this woman was malevolent and unstable. I just thought, *It's my fault. I should have pulled more weeds.*

4

When I was twelve, letters from my father began to arrive with the tedious frequency of junk mail. On lined paper folded over itself in three rectangles, he explained how ill he was when he bashed my mother and my sisters. 'It was my manic depression.' 'I wasn't taking my medication.' 'I wasn't going to church.'

He sent me a birthday card when I was thirteen. On the cover was an image of the night sky and, in garish purple letters, the message *Shoot for the moon because even if you miss you'll land among the stars*. Inside he wrote that he loved me, signed his name with a sequence of x's and o's, and enclosed two scratchies which turned out to be losers.

I never responded to his letters, in which he spoke of his pride at being my father, of my status as a son, the only son. I skimmed the words like they were instructions for a school exam. There was nothing my father could do for me. He could do nothing to help me. Reading his pleading letters, responding to them, was useless. A waste of my time.

A part of me enjoyed holding this ruthlessness inside me, of being unreachable to him. I hoped that he was suffering, that it upset him his son didn't write back. I hated my father and my family for landing me here in foster care, with Tracey.

My mother's side of my family reached out to me too, with Nan one day inviting Jacinta and me to visit. While we were there, I asked her why she didn't take Jacinta and me in, already knowing the answer.

'We were terrified of your father.' A gold filling in her mouth gleamed. 'Barry was a very violent man.'

'I wish you had taken us,' I said weakly.

'I wish we could have.'

That was it then. It couldn't have been otherwise.

I looked around at her nice, clean house, felt a fever of rage. I felt pathetic sitting here. What was the point of visiting this woman, who may as well have been a stranger? She wasn't my family, just an old woman who wanted to assuage her guilt for an afternoon. This wasn't about us. This was about her. Whatever family meant, she had failed to be it. Family was only a useless word.

A month later, Tracey squawked for me to come to the kitchen. I got up off the lounge where I was playing *Pokémon* on my Game Boy and went to her. She sat at the chintzy kitchen table, steam from her coffee cup meandering above the newspaper spread on the table.

'Yes, Tracey?' She ignored me and continued reading. 'Yes, Tracey?' I said again, to no response.

This was a game she played: ask you to come to her, which you would do, then sit in silence for two or three minutes, ignoring you so completely you started to wonder if you'd gone mad and only imagined her calling for you. If you got upset, she'd lambast you for your lack of patience. Express too much frustration and you'd be made to sit in the corner of the kitchen as punishment. The trick was to wait her out, until she became bored, until she finally said, 'I'd like you to hang out the washing,' or 'Can you chop some carrots for dinner?'

I stood waiting silently, concentrating on the pale skin of her forehead.

Finally, she spoke without looking up. 'The Department wants to know if you'd like to see your father?'

'Yeah, I'd like that,' I said.

She licked her thumb then used it to turn to the next page of the newspaper. I shuffled on the spot, trying to get her attention nonverbally, a method that had not yet been prohibited. She continued to read for a minute without acknowledging I was still beside her, until at last she said, 'You can go now.'

The elevator hummed as somebody came up. The silver doors wobbled then peeled open, releasing a balding, pot-bellied man wearing a Hawaiian shirt, shorts and thongs.

'Corey,' the man said. 'It's me. Dad.'

I looked at the fat mess of a man. He was unrecognisable from the tall, slim and powerful man I'd known as my father. Dorian Gray's portrait halfway through. The years had beaten the shit out of him and you could smell the blood.

'Hi, Dad,' I said to the walking pudding. It gobbled up the metres between us. I stood and then his arms were around me, pressing hard, desperate.

The social worker chimed in. 'If you want to come with me to the room.'

We shuffled through a hallway into a stark white room and sat opposite each other at a round black table, the only furniture in the room. The social worker pulled a chair from the table into the corner and sat there. 'Okay,' she said, 'pretend I'm not here for the next hour.'

My father shook his head. 'I can't spend an hour alone with my son?'

'Barry,' she cooed, 'we discussed this. It's just how it has to be.'

'Fucking hell,' he growled.

The social worker's face paled.

'Bullshit,' he hissed before he remembered his powerlessness. 'Don't worry, I'll be good.' He gave her a thumbs up and smiled yellow.

The blob looked at me. 'It's good to see you, son.'

'Yeah, it's good to see you too.'

Was this mess even my father? Was this some trick Tracey was pulling?

We talked. In circles, we came back again and again to the same subject.

'I was ill, son. You have to understand. I was ill.' He seemed slow. Was he like this when I was young and I just didn't notice? He picked up on my thoughts and explained that he'd had a brain aneurysm a few years before.

I'd become bothered by what he did to my mother and my sisters. It seemed wrong to me then, in a way it never did when I was a child.

'Why didn't you take your medication?' I asked him.

'Because I was sick, I didn't think I needed it.'

Despite myself, I could see the logic.

I asked him about my mother. Sometimes I thought about her, daydreaming of life with her instead of with Tracey.

'How did you and Mum fall in love?'

He couldn't remember. 'It just kind of happened,' he said, my thirteen-year-old romantic fantasies deflating.

Over the next year, I saw my father several more times. Eventually we were allowed to sit on a bench in the park opposite the Department building without a social worker present. Duck shit was everywhere and the whole place smelled awful, but my father was chuffed they trusted him. He smiled without revealing his teeth, lips pressed together, which lent him an air of cheekiness.

'What have you been up to?' I asked him one day.

'Watching a lot of movies,' he said, smiling lovingly.

'Any good ones?'

'Oh yeah, I saw this good one. I forget the name.'

'What was it about?'

He struggled to explain the plot, rambling for a minute but seeming happy with what he had said.

I looked at him, disgust surging through me.

———

The next time Tracey asked if I'd like to see my father, I told her that I wouldn't.

I was done with him. He sent a few letters asking why I didn't want to meet him any more but I never answered. I told myself I was doing it for my mother, but I didn't really believe that.

Sometimes Tracey took us to stay with her country music friends on weekends, women with hyphenated first names and men missing front teeth. The adults took turns singing covers of Slim Dusty and Keith Urban, or trying out their invariably terrible originals.

While all this took place, the dozen or so children who'd been dragged along, like dogs to a vacuum cleaner convention, would try to put as much distance as possible between us and the saccharine melancholy of the adults.

Once we'd hidden ourselves away to play video games when Kylie tried to cut in on my turn.

'Fuck off,' I said, holding her back.

'I'm telling Mum,' she cried and stormed off.

I kept playing *Tony Hawk*.

'Corey,' I heard Tracey say from behind me.

'Yes?'

I could smell Tracey's perfume, feel her body enclose me from behind as she snatched the PlayStation controller up out of my hands.

'What did I do wrong?'

'Kylie said you were being selfish.'

'It was my turn. Her turn is next.'

I felt her arms underneath my armpits, pinching the skin as she pulled me up.

'Ouch!'

'Oh, don't be a little sook. Get up.'

'You're not supposed to touch us foster kids,' I said, my face inches from hers.

'Shut up,' she spat. She dragged me downstairs, out of the house and into the car, while everyone came to watch.

'You can stay here until you've calmed down,' Tracey taunted, before she and the others filed back into the house.

The car was boiling so I hopped out and sat on the nature strip. I was very thirsty. I swallowed the saliva that was left in my mouth, sucked my cheeks dry of all their moisture.

Tracey came out and told me to get back in the car. 'I didn't give you permission to leave.'

'But it's boiling in there!'

She told me again to get back in and I had no choice but to comply.

I don't know how long I stayed in the car but I was certain I was going to die. I thought about news stories of babies baking in cars as their mothers played pokie machines. I was fourteen and considered how embarrassing it would be if I died like that.

Finally, after hours in the car, Tracey and the rest of the kids came out and we started to drive home. I stared at the back of her seat and I wanted to kill her. I wanted to rip every hair out of her head. I wanted to pour boiling coffee all over her stomach. I wanted to flush her head in the toilet. I wanted to piss in her eyes.

When we arrived home, everyone rushed to get out of the car.

'Corey!' I turned away from the door to face Tracey behind me. 'You're not going in the house yet. You'll stay out here in the garage.'

'Can I get a drink first and go to the toilet?'

'Nope,' she said, in a chirpy, sadistic way.

I found myself screaming. 'Fuck you! I want food and water!'

'Yelling won't help,' she said calmly, confidently, turning her back on me. It infuriated me that she wasn't even scared that I was yelling. Was that how small I was to her?

'You're a fucking cunt!'

'Keep going on like that, mate, and you'll be living in a tent in the backyard.' The door slammed shut behind her.

I thumped the door with my fists. A second later, it swung open and Tracey was standing there, nostrils flared, wispy blonde hair bleached white in the sun that slanted in through the carport. For an instant, I thought she might take pity on me. I hadn't had water or food for a long time.

'That's another two hours,' she announced imperiously, shutting the door in my face again.

My body was so hot with hate I thought I was going to die. I clenched my fists, digging my fingernails into my palms. I wanted to snap my own hands off and show them to Tracey. I wanted to show my rage to her in the form of my own mutilation. I felt angrier and more humiliated than I'd ever been.

At the time of my explosion, I could not articulate why I was exploding. Now I can. I had finally recognised, in some wordless, animalistic way, that pleasing Tracey was impossible. There was no set of principles I could abide by that would win me peace. She was sick and no amount of punishment or humiliation she inflicted on me could ever cure her. Tracey would always be cruel.

I found a broom leaning against where the rubbish bins were kept in the carport and walked around to the front door of the house. I hit it against the screen door. Again and again and again. I put all my strength into it. Tracey appeared, sliding open the glass door behind the screen one.

'What are you doing, Corey?'

'I fucking hate you! Slut! Cunt! I'll kill you!' Tears and snot were running down my face and I felt like I could go on bashing the screen door forever. For the first time ever, I saw fear in Tracey's eyes. I was bigger than her now, just. Despite not having enough food, I had grown. It spurred me on, seeing her flinch as the metal screen wobbled and warped under my assault. I dropped the broom and began to slap the metal with my palms and kick it with my feet.

'Corey, stop,' Tracey said softly.

'I'm gonna kill you,' I screamed, feeling my jaw morph, feeling my whole body turn into nothing. The words came out of my mouth twisted, gargled. 'I hate you!' Kylie and Sarah appeared behind Tracey. They smirked at my self-abasement. Tracey ushered them away.

She slid the glass door closed and stepped out of my sight. I slapped my now-raw hands against the metal screen a few more times.

I knelt down on the concrete, panting, suddenly feeling small and pathetic again. I stared at the screen door, still in place, as though nothing had happened. Anger returned at the thought of its own uselessness. I crossed my legs, shuffled closer to the screen door and resumed slamming my hands against it. Five years of pent-up hate, despair and pain were finally being released. When all the strength had gone in my arms, I got on my back and kicked with my feet until they failed too. And then I let out one last scream. 'I hate you!'

I lay on the concrete, exhausted, my hands and feet on fire from striking the metal, my throat from screaming.

What had I done? Terror replaced fury. She was going to punish me severely for my outburst. She was going to punish me like she hadn't punished any of us before. What I had done was far beyond the pale of any tantrums any of us had thrown.

I decided I had to leave Tracey's house, more from fear of what my punishment would be than from principle. There was no turning back.

I knew where I had to go. I got to my feet and limped around to the side of the house, to the garden hose. I tore it off the tap, which I turned on and let fill my mouth with water, swallowing until my belly was swollen.

I hobbled for a few kilometres, until I felt my stomach cramping. I stopped at a service station, desperately needing to take a massive shit.

I waddled to the front counter, like a duck with diarrhoea. 'Can I get the key to your toilet?' I whispered.

'Yeah, mate,' came the response from the teenager behind the counter, who was not much older than me.

He handed me the key, and, clenching the blessed metal, I limped out of the icy-cool service station, down the oily driveway and to a white door peeling like sunburn. As I opened the door, the smell of truck-driver faeces hit me. I slammed the door shut, quiveringly stripped my pants to my ankles and sat down.

I think that was the best shit of my life. I had seen *The Shawshank*

Redemption recently in school and I kept thinking of that scene where Andy Dufresne climbs out of the sewage pipe and raises his arms in the torrential downpour in liberation. I enjoyed the slop bucketing out of me. It seemed metaphysical. A sign that my life was about to change, signified by a brown rainbow coiling upon itself. I must have sat on that toilet for an hour. When I returned the key to the console operator he gave me a look of surprise, as if he'd completely forgotten about me.

I limped along the main road for a while then crossed into suburbia, trying to remember the way.

Teenagers slouched on street corners, straddling pushbikes as they took stabbing drags on cigarettes. I quickened my pace in the remaining sunlight. It was a dangerous area.

I kept looking over my shoulder expecting Tracey to pull up in the station wagon. As if somehow she'd know where I was. After years under her thumb, I'd come to impute virtual omniscience to her. The thought that kept going through my head was that she would somehow know exactly when to drive down the street and cut me off. I was on the verge of vomiting from adrenaline, even as I told myself, 'She hasn't found me, she can't find me, she won't find me.' I dreaded the uber-punishment she would have in store for me if I was caught. Sarah and Mikayla had run away before and they'd suffered month-long groundings, even though she'd tracked them down quickly. My escape had gone beyond two hours.

I picked up a large branch that had fallen from a tree and held it in case I needed to use it against her.

Finally, I arrived at Cathy Cowan's house, where Jacinta still lived. I rapped on the front door and my sister appeared. 'Corey!' she cried, engulfing me with her arms. She was ten now, tall and thin. She looked so different.

'I need water,' I said into her blonde hair. She led me inside and the stench of the house filled my nostrils. 'Cathy! Corey's here.' I strode to the sink and put my mouth to the tap, drinking until my belly hurt, not caring about the cockroaches I knew had crawled all over it.

I walked into the dim lounge room where Cathy sat in her rocking chair, like always, a jumbo glass of watered-down Scotch beside her.

'Hello, son,' she croaked. 'What brings you here?'

'I've run away from Tracey's house.' I caught her up on events in a blizzard of fresh anger.

Cathy listened attentively, and when I was done she told me she was sorry. 'You've had a big day. Would you like some lollies?' Her belly folded as she fumbled for the giant lolly jar beside her ashtray, unscrewed the lid and thrust it out with her mottled, spindly arm.

I plunged my hand into it, my fingers a dragnet of greed. I sat on the couch, unwinding caramel eclairs, and told her about how I hadn't eaten food for more than twenty-four hours. Cathy put some sausage rolls in the oven.

The phone rang later in the evening. Cathy picked it up and glanced at me. 'Hi, Tracey.'

'Don't tell her I'm here,' I mouthed.

She nodded. 'Sorry,' said Cathy, a fraction too loud. 'Corey isn't here.'

Despite hearing Cathy cover for me, I didn't fully trust her. The higher tone of her voice when she said I wasn't here might have been a pre-arranged code to indicate I *was*. I ducked out of the room and carefully cracked the back door open. It would be my way out of the house if Cathy and Tracey were conspiring to trap me. I padded back into the lounge room just as Cathy finished up on the phone.

'Tracey doesn't think you're here.'

'Okay,' I said, warily.

The next day a social worker came to the house. She sat down on the armchair beside Cathy, holding a cup of water she'd chosen over the glass of Scotch Cathy had offered her.

'Tracey is prepared to take you back if you'd like.'

'I'm not going back. No way.'

'You could stay here and live with Jacinta if you'd like?'

I looked around the dingy lounge room, with the brown nicotine stains on the walls. I looked at Jacinta, absentmindedly doing colouring-in on the carpet. I knew the fact she was my sister should mean something, that it should make me want to live here, but it didn't. I didn't care about family. My parents had taught me how sacred family was. Blood meant nothing to people like us.

I told the social worker I wanted to live somewhere else.

'I'm sorry, Cathy,' I said, not wanting to hurt her feelings. 'I just think it's best if I find somewhere else to live.'

'That's okay, mate. You've gotta do what you've gotta do.'

'Okay,' the social worker sighed. 'Are you sure?'

I knew it would be less hassle for the social worker if I stayed put, but if I said no to this place surely they had to listen. 'I don't want to live here,' I reiterated.

———

Tracey was my guardian devil. I was redeemed by her viciousness and despotism. I know it more deeply than my name.

You're not supposed to think there's anything good about suffering, but I do. Tracey broke me and I'm grateful she did. Her cruelty saved me from becoming a monster. Or it made me a weaker monster at least. For four long years, Tracey dismantled me piece by piece, destroyed a boy who believed he was invincible, a raging, violent boy who believed only in power. I know what that boy would have grown up to be. After Tracey, I had no interest in talking to anyone, let alone fighting them. I no longer believed I deserved the world. I didn't think I deserved anything.

Self-hate was better and safer than the free-floating anger and violence and selfishness it had replaced. What occurred under Tracey – mind games, hunger, rape, loneliness, abasement – crushed me. But it took being stripped of my humanity for me to gain humanity. Without this, I think I would have become my father. He made me one way, Tracey made me another.

I think back to what that boy had done. Hitting his mother and sisters, choking children almost to death, throwing chairs at teachers. Tracey was my penance.

That's not to say there weren't other ways I could have been changed. Therapy, love, kindness. But cruelty can also save.

Why do I feel grateful to her? Why do I fear the man I would have become if I hadn't entered her house? Why do I remember the nights she spent in internet chat rooms talking to men? Why do I think about the boyfriends she had brief relationships with and who invariably left her? Why do I remember the way she would sometimes look so sad? Why do I remember a breast cancer scare she had?

The boy who went into her house did not care about things like this. The things she did to me – did they make me care?

I believe they did.

5

We drove through streets that all looked the same. Identical brick houses built cheap by the Government for people who could not survive independently.

The social worker parked. 'This is it,' she said. We got out of the car and made our way along a path through a leafy, ordered yard teeming with constellations of colourful flowers nurtured for years, a stark contrast to the failed gardens in the rest of the street. We came to a little verandah and rapped on the door.

'Just a moment,' a woman sang. The door opened and a squat, curly-haired woman stood smiling at me. 'Hello, I'm Helen.'

'I'm Corey,' I said politely, feeling like a puppy in a pet shop, as the social worker introduced herself beside me.

'Lovely to meet you both. Come in. I'll give you the grand tour.'

It was a tiny house. To the left of the doorway was a small lounge room, to the right an even smaller dining room containing five unmatched chairs dwarfing a wooden table. I wasn't sure if people could sit at the table since the walls around it were lined with tall chipboard shelves overflowing with books, magazines and papers.

Helen led us past this. 'Here's the kitchen,' she commanded proudly. I looked around at a space barely larger than the car we'd driven here in. White walls and a ceiling, and benches decorated in a lime-green laminate. I sniffed the air and detected the faint scent of dishwashing liquid, a sign of cleanliness.

We moved on to the bathroom. Even smaller than the kitchen, I took in everything at a single glance: the sink, a mirrored medicine cabinet affixed to the wall and a dual shower-bathtub, all revealed by murky light from a puny frosted glass window.

Each time Helen stopped to show us a new room, I'd nod and say, 'Nice.' Being courteous increased my chances of her taking me. Nobody had told me this, but it seemed obvious.

After I examined and complimented the toilet, we shuffled down a dim hallway, off which four bedrooms extended. There was Helen's room, one for her daughter Amanda and her foster daughter Chantelle, another for her two daughters Fiona and Megan. The last belonged to her son, Andrew, and me, if I came to live here.

'Nice,' I said again.

As Helen led us back down the hallway, I decided I could accept living here. The house, while cramped and gloomy, was not dirty. That was good enough. I had to get out of Cathy Cowan's house, and if I said no to this placement then there'd only be another one of these awkward inspections. I was already dreading sitting down at the table in the claustrophobic dining room, where I'd seen a sleeve of biscuits and a jug of juice. We'd have a 'chat' for what would feel like the length of an old black-and-white film, pretending that I wasn't a child who needed a place to live and so was making myself the cutest, friendliest thing in the world.

'There's one last thing I have to show you,' Helen said mysteriously, opening a screen door at the rear of the house and disappearing. We followed her outside to the backyard, into an oasis with grass so green that at first I thought it was fake. Around the perimeter ran a curling garden of rose bushes and banksias and manicured shrubs, sunflowers striving upwards against the brick exterior of the house. In the centre of the emerald lawn, at the heart of the haven, beneath the shade of a huge tree rich with foliage, sat an ornate white table and two chairs.

'It's beautiful, isn't it?' beamed Helen.

'It's very pretty,' I said in my best voice, wondering how hard she worked the kids to maintain it.

Inside, we squeezed around the dining table for juice and biscuits. I gorged myself in as slow and dignified a way as I could. I'd been trying to eat as little as possible at Cathy Cowan's house, conscious of the ever-present cockroaches and insects.

'You have so many books here,' the social worker remarked, running a hand across a bookcase.

'I love to read,' said Helen. 'Do you like to read, Corey?'

'Yeah,' I smiled.

'Well, there's enough books here to keep you reading for years,' she said, returning the smile.

On the drive back, I asked the social worker whether she thought Helen would take me.

'It's up to her.'

'I was good, wasn't I?'

'Yes, you were. We'll see what happens.'

After a few days spent hovering anxiously by the phone, the Department called to say Helen had said yes. I'd passed the test. I was acceptable.

I gave the handset back to Cathy who looked at me from her chair. 'Are you sure you don't want to live here? Jacinta would love it if you stayed.'

Cathy seemed hurt that I was going. I didn't want to upset her, but couldn't she see the state her house was in? Couldn't she smell it? Something golden was in me – smaller, duller than before, but still there. This place would coat it in filth, dim it, kill it.

I mumbled an explanation.

The social worker was to arrive in a few hours so I quickly gathered the few belongings I had.

'See you, Jacinta,' I said, hugging her on the front porch.

'Don't go, brother,' she pleaded, clinging to me. 'Can't you live with us?'

I looked at her face, her brown eyes the same as mine.

'I'm sorry,' I said. 'I have to go.'

'Why?'

I noticed lice crawling through her blonde hair. 'I just do.'

As we reversed out of the driveway, Jacinta and Cathy stood on the verandah waving. Was I doing the right thing? Should I have stayed? The car rolled out onto the bitumen road and Jacinta trotted down the stairs and started jogging towards us. The social worker straightened the car as Jacinta caught us, slapping the roof with her hand. I rolled my window down and Jacinta leaned in to cuddle me. 'I'll miss you.'

'I'll miss you too,' I said, gently untangling myself from her.

I settled into Helen's house. She was kind. Her children and even Chantelle, the other foster kid, had great affection for her. They hugged and kissed her, fixed her cups of tea.

Helen fed us well. For breakfast, we could choose between toast, cereal or fruit salad. For school lunches, Helen did up brown paper bags with a banana, apple and pear in them, a muesli bar and two sandwiches stuffed with chicken, lettuce, cheese and mayonnaise. For dinner, there was meat and veg, oven-cooked frozen pizzas, occasionally take-away Chinese.

Helen's kidneys had gone kaput and she received dialysis several times a week. On those days, when I arrived home from school Amanda or Chantelle would shush me at the front door. 'Helen's asleep, be quiet.'

Because of her illness, Helen couldn't work and money was tight. She took a newspaper delivery route and we all chipped in to help. On Saturday mornings, we would pick up a stack of local newspapers, pamphlets, flyers and brochures, and Saturday afternoons were spent with everyone in the house occupying every available inch of sitting space in the living room to package the material. We placed a copy of the week's newspaper down first then topped it with promotional materials before rolling the stack into a tight cylinder, twisting a rubber band around the top and sliding it down to the middle of the thick bundle. It was laborious work which left my fingers and palms black with ink, but with the whole family sitting around the lounge room I felt a part of something. On Sunday mornings we walked the streets placing them in letterboxes across the suburb.

And, as it turned out, Helen, despite her illness, never requested assistance from us children with her garden. Instead, it was something she sought quietude in, a solitary communion. She seemed to find peace in it. The other kids loved her and would often volunteer to help, not out of duress but an earnest desire to help her.

Having shifted suburbs to live with Helen, I changed high schools.

On my first day at the new school, I didn't know how to make friends. At lunch time, I borrowed a book on medieval warfare and sat on a bench hidden around a corner from the library. For the first few weeks, I spent every break sitting there reading about trebuchets. For some reason, I wasn't mercilessly bullied. Possibly because other kids were scared I might snap and come to school with a trebuchet.

My days dragged by, sitting on the same bench, feeling alone and friendless, until one morning tea a girl with peroxide-blonde hair said hello to me.

'What are you doing by yourself?' she asked.

'Just reading.' I held up the book. 'About castles.'

'You can come sit over with us,' she said, pointing to a group of kids, so I did. They took me in and, slowly, became my friends. Gradually, I was becoming less alone.

I also joined the local chess club where each Wednesday night I duked it out with other players. Chess consumed me. I enjoyed the fact you only had yourself to rely on. The only trust required of you was trust in yourself, your powers of calculation. There was no randomness in it; you determined your own destiny.

Chess illuminated the mathematics that imbues the world. For the first time, I could see patterns. Things at last made sense. Here was something where you were in control. You decided what moves you made, what your strategy was. Your opponent could blunder but theoretically you could play perfectly. Now I played chess properly. If you were disciplined enough, if you saw further than your opponent, you would win.

I wasn't the best player, but it gave me something to obsess about, lent my life a focus. While other teenagers sculled vodka at house parties, I studied the Sicilian Defence. While boys pleaded for blow jobs, I solved checkmate puzzles. Chess granted me a sense of purpose, shielding me from alcohol, drugs and any attention from teenage girls.

My ego reinflated. Alienation was replaced by a feeling of superiority. I was better than other people. I played *chess*.

Helen had a boyfriend, Pat, who looked like Tarzan: tall and tanned with long unruly brown hair. I liked the starkness of him. The smell of cigarettes that clung to him, the split ends of his hair, the faded and hole-riddled singlets, the bushes of his underarm hair. He lived in his own house across town, a spartan dive with dirty magazines on the lounge room coffee table of naked women bent over motorcycles and quad bikes.

Pat was a throwback to earlier times. He scorned modernity. He'd find me in my bedroom playing computer games and growl, 'The screen is bad for you. A boy should be in the sun.'

'A little bit isn't going to hurt, is it?' I'd say, and he'd mutter something about rickets.

Pat had lived a hard life. He was uneducated to the point Helen had to read out any letters sent to him. Pat had spent years working with the only thing he had of value: his body. It had taken a toll on him and he was plagued with back and shoulder pain. I'd heard snatches of conversations between him and Helen about his childhood, suggestions of violence, allusions to abuse.

Pat worked as a furniture removalist for a charity, Save the Children, and when school holidays arrived I spent two weeks volunteering with him. Helen had suggested it would help build my resume for a job. She had told me I needed to begin preparing for leaving foster care. 'The Department will not be there for you when you turn eighteen. You'll have to look after yourself,' she said. 'You're fourteen, it's not that far away.'

On my first day, Pat arrived early in his aquamarine ute.

'Ready for a hard day's work?' he said, fixing coffee for himself and Helen.

'Yeah, should be good,' I said, eager to take on responsibility.

We hopped in the ute and drove to the Save the Children shop where we were to deliver furniture people had purchased, following which we'd pick up things people were donating to the shop.

We worked through the morning, lugging washing machines and fridges and couches and televisions out of apartments and houses, staggering to the ute before securing them in the tray with hockey straps.

'I'm buggered,' Pat panted, doubled over, as we broke for lunch. He dug his hand into his pocket and fetched a cigarette from its packet, shoving it between his lips and lighting it with a click of his lighter. 'That's better,' he coughed, straightening up before another hacking fit hit him.

'Should you be smoking?' I asked, but he pretended not to hear me.

That afternoon, while we sat in the ute outside the shop awaiting instructions for our next job, Pat turned down the radio and looked at me.

'How do you like working?' he asked.

'It's good,' I said.

'It's good for you to be with people, isn't it?'

'I guess.'

'Gotta stay away from screens. They'll rot your brain,' he commanded.

When we had unloaded the last of the furniture at the Save the Children shop and were on our way to Helen's house, I asked Pat what he'd do that night.

'Gonna drink cold beer in the backyard,' he grinned.

I admired the purity of his life. He had boiled it down to labouring, cigarettes, beer and loving Helen. This formula yielded everything he needed. He required nothing else.

I knew I wanted more than Pat. What it was, though, I couldn't say.

Building on my experience with Pat, I soon got a job cleaning a small factory in an industrial estate across town. Peter's Fine European

Smallgoods was owned and operated by Peter, who'd immigrated from Germany when he was a teenager.

Spatters of pink meat coated the walls, stainless steel benches and concrete floor. It seemed an impossible task to clean all the meat.

'It usually takes me about half an hour to do,' he said, giving me a quick demonstration.

I walked home that first night drenched from the hose, raw meat clinging to the hair of my forearms and calves. I felt proud to be working. The dirtier I got, the more heroic I felt.

I was a foster kid. When my back was against the wall, I continued to fight.

This was a trick I had learned to dampen down pain, to mythologise myself. By making myself something more than human, suffering no longer reduced me but made me grow.

Twice a week, on Mondays and Thursdays, I rode my bike from school to the factory, changed clothes in the cold room, and began. What took Peter thirty minutes took me four hours.

After a month, when I was still there at 7.30 at night, Peter said, 'Mate, you should be faster by now.'

'I'm sorry.'

'I need to lock up,' he said. 'Don't you want to go home?'

Not really, I wanted to say. To be honest, I preferred cleaning stale meat alone in the factory. At least I was being paid. It was meditative too. I enjoyed going into a quiet zone of scrubbing with no thoughts in my mind, the repetitive action of holding a hose over a section of wall or metal sausage rack and then scrubbing the dirt and filth away.

And things had started going badly at Helen's house. She had taken issue with my 'isolating behaviours'. She thought I wasn't getting involved with the family enough, that I spent too much time in my room playing video games. I attempted to spend more time in the lounge room, the only common area of the house, watching TV with everyone. Yet my mere physical presence wasn't enough.

One evening Helen had said to me, 'Why are you sulking?'

I didn't think I was sulking. Was I sulking? I had been thinking about schoolwork, girls, the deep thoughts of a fourteen-year-old boy.

'Just go to your room if you're going to sulk,' she said, dismissing me.

'I don't think I was sulking?' I said, unsure of how to defuse the situation. I had been sitting on the couch daydreaming.

'You are sulking,' said Andrew.

'I'm sorry, but I honestly didn't think I was sulking.'

'Just go to your room,' Andrew commanded.

I awkwardly left the room, confused. Was something wrong with my face? I'd read about alien hand syndrome, in which a person's hand would move independently of their will. Did I have alien face syndrome? Was my face, independent of my will, adopting the crestfallen quality of a baby robbed of candy?

I had to get to the bottom of these accusations of sulking. I grabbed my towel off the back of my bedroom door and headed for the shower. I looked at my face in the mirror which was speckled with a few flecks of toothpaste from the maniacal rituals of Chantelle, who brushed her teeth a dozen times a day. She was always smiling, partly out of friendliness, partly from a supreme pride in her gleaming white smile, and, I thought, partly from her slight learning disability.

I let my face assume its resting position. Was the default state of my face a sulk? I didn't think so, yet this was the facial configuration that was causing so much trouble. It had to go. I examined my face in the mirror, experimenting with different ways of holding my lips and eyebrows, until I found a half-smile that I thought suggested deep inner contentment.

Unfortunately, this facial innovation was not well received.

'Why are you smirking?' Helen asked me that night following dinner, as I sat watching television with the family.

Cleaning Peter's Fine European Smallgoods factory didn't require changing myself. I liked the solitude, just me and the meat and the water. Immersed in it, soaked and squalid, I felt okay. It was honest work, there was no need to pretend to be someone you weren't in order to make other people comfortable. For a few hours, my world narrowed down to nothing outside of a little factory, four connected rooms filled with smoking racks and mince machines and knives and hooks and paprika on chopping boards, and all I had to do to succeed was to clean it. That was the sole metric: was it clean?

Peter was a handsome guy. A succession of ultra-beautiful women arrived at the factory. I'd see them walking up the gravel driveway to the stairs out back which led up to his home. Occasionally, Peter would show one of the women through the factory, boasting of his business success.

'That's Corey,' he'd say, pointing at the sopping goblin sweeping fleshy offcuts into a drain. I'd wave and say hello.

Inevitably, during a tour Peter would hold a bratwurst up and ask the woman, 'Would you like some sausage?' They'd giggle and draw closer to their witty, financially successful man.

'We better leave Corey to work,' Peter would say.

'Goodbye,' waved the wet goblin.

Shortly after, I'd hear the moaning from Peter's apartment upstairs, the bed legs like pistons through the ceiling. I found it funny, the contrast of their afternoon delight and my filthy labour. The unimaginable glory above and the terrible muck below.

One afternoon, I was in my room playing games on my computer when Helen knocked on the door and came to sit on my bed. 'Corey, I wanted to talk to you.'

I paused the game to speak with her. 'Sure thing. What's up?'

'I think you're playing too many video games.'

'It's only a couple of hours a night,' I said. 'I'm doing my chores and I'm doing my homework and getting good marks in school.'

'Yes, but you need to be a part of this family,' she said.

Jesus Christ, I thought. 'I'm trying to be a part of the family. What more do I need to do? Can you tell me exactly what you'd like me to do to please you?'

'Corey,' she said, a little offended. 'Being part of a family is not a cake recipe. There's no list of rules you can just follow and everything will be fine. You have to engage with us.'

So it wasn't about whether I was good enough; it was about her feelings. Whether she *felt* I was part of the family. I swallowed anger, reminded of the way I'd laboured to satisfy Tracey's shifting sense of being obeyed. This was a cousin of that, I thought.

'I'll come out of my room more,' I promised, hate in my throat.

Helen thanked me in a clipped way and left the room.

The following night, when I returned from work, I greeted Helen but she ignored me.

'Helen?'

Helen sat silently engrossed in the book she was reading.

Andrew looked up at me from the armchair beside his mother. 'Mum doesn't want to talk to you.'

'What have I done wrong?'

Andrew sighed a great patriarchal sigh. 'We've tried so hard to include you but you just don't seem to want to be a part of this family.'

'I'm trying my best,' I said, looking between Helen and Andrew. This was absurd, communicating with a grown woman through her son.

I didn't understand what I had done wrong. I hadn't yelled or been violent. I'd tried to include myself more.

'I'm sorry, Helen,' I said, willing her to look at me, to acknowledge I was standing before her.

She continued reading without looking up. I gazed at Andrew, who was absorbed in reading too.

'Helen? Andrew?'

Nothing.

'Okay,' I said and went and showered.

The next day, halfway through the final class at school, I was called into the office. A social worker was examining a corkboard in the waiting area.

'Hello?' I said.

'Hi, Corey,' she replied, straightening. 'I'm here to take you to your new foster care placement.'

'Can I talk to Helen?' I asked.

'Helen doesn't want contact with you.'

I felt a bittersweet satisfaction. I was right again. People couldn't be trusted. I asked the social worker where I'd live now.

'There's a family who will take you for a little while.'

Fifteen minutes later, we were walking across the scraggly lawn of a dilapidated house, my new foster home.

A woman named Karen greeted us and ushered us inside.

I introduced myself, feeling like a salesman desperate to close the deal.

'I'm Roger,' said a thin man, emerging from the kitchen behind Karen. He patted his palms dry with a tea towel and shook my hand.

'I have to get going back to the office,' said the social worker. 'Everything okay here now?'

'Yes,' said Karen.

I was momentarily panicked by being left alone within minutes of arriving, with the length of this placement unclear, but I decided that protesting would be futile.

Karen showed me to a bedroom where my belongings had already been sent from Helen's house in three neat boxes. She excused herself and left me to unpack, shutting the door behind her.

I sat on the new bed. Within the space of an hour, I'd learned I'd been rejected by Helen and moved into a new foster home. I wondered what Roger and Karen would want from me. Would they want obedience like Tracey or love like Helen?

To my surprise and relief, it turned out they wanted neither.

After I'd organised my room, I trundled to the dining table where the biological children – Chelsea, eight, Anna, eleven, David, thirteen, and Liam, sixteen – were already sitting. Roger introduced me to them briefly and then I ate in silence while they discussed their days and bickered and laughed. When I'd finished my meal, I took my plate to the sink and returned to my room.

I felt invisible, which was fine by me.

I was the only foster child there. I stayed out of their way. After school, I walked to my room, closed the door and lay in bed. Before I knew it, the sky would grow dark and dinner would be served. Then I'd go back to my room and fall asleep.

On weekends, they jetted off to family functions without inviting me. I'd pop my head out of my room to find the house empty. This was paradise to me. It felt honest and nice. How liberating it was to not have to concern myself with whether I had resting sulk face.

Gradually, though, the initial indifference to my presence in the house became hostility. I took to my room more and more. I would stare at the ceiling for hours, lost inside myself. I wished something would happen to rescue me from all this.

———

'Mum, when's Corey moving out?' Chelsea asked.

'Soon, baby,' Karen said.

From between her mother's legs, she gave me a look of disdain so withering I wanted to disappear on the spot. I didn't show how much I was hurt and remained sitting in the lounge room, pretending I hadn't heard the exchange. After about twenty minutes, I stood up from the couch and casually sauntered to my bedroom. I closed the door behind me and fell onto my bed and cried.

I didn't feel any anger, no impulse to resist this casual cruelty. I hated myself so deeply it seemed a given people around me would attack me.

And I was frightened about what the future held. I was fifteen now. What would I do when I turned eighteen? I didn't belong anywhere.

A few months into my placement, the Department assigned a new social worker to me, Melisa. I still remember her pale skin and the faded freckles that dotted her thin face. Black hair, green eyes. She was different to other social workers. When we met, it felt like she was listening. She asked me how I was going, put her hand underneath my chin when I couldn't make eye contact.

'You're getting good marks at school,' she said to me one day when we met in a park near the Department offices, as she held up a report card from my most recent semester.

'I guess so,' I said.

'There's no guessing about it,' she smiled.

'Okay.'

'So the question I wanted to ask you is: what do you want to do when you leave care?' she asked.

I glanced away at people walking their dogs around us. I'd started to hate looking people in the eye. I was frightened of seeing disgust. I knew I was revolting and stupid, but I preferred not to have it confirmed, to read it in their irises and pupils.

I thought about what would happen to me when I left care. I'd always wanted to do something important and exciting, but lately I'd stopped dreaming.

I told Melisa I didn't know what I'd do.

'Well,' she said, pausing to reach down into a tote bag she'd brought and placing a blue folder on the table. 'Have a look at this.'

'What is it?'

'It's a prospectus for a boarding school, Nudgee College.'

I rotated the folder with my hand and scrutinised it. There was a photograph of teenage boys in smart blue-and-white stripe blazers strolling along a garden path. Above it there was a stylised emblem superimposed on the images, with a Latin motto: *Signum Fidei.*

'What does *Signum Fidei* mean?' I asked.

'I don't know.'

I admired the thick, glossy material.

'It looks pretty cool,' I said.

'Would you like to go there?' Melisa asked.

'Of course,' I said.

'I'm going to make that happen, okay. You deserve a good education, Corey.'

I knew I shouldn't trust Melisa, that she was just another social worker, one more in a long line of bureaucrats who'd failed to keep promises. And yet she sounded so genuine I couldn't help but feel hopeful. That or I was desperate enough to believe anything.

Liam and I swung our school bags to the lounge room floor and sank into armchairs, continuing the strange fight he had picked on our walk home. It was a ridiculous spat about the meaning of the term 'free-to-air television'. He claimed it meant networks didn't have to pay to use the broadcast spectrum, while I said it meant people didn't have to pay to view it.

'You're so fucking stupid,' he shouted. 'I'm right, you idiot.'

Frightened by his disproportionate anger, I said, 'Let's just agree to disagree.'

He suddenly jumped up from his chair on the other side of the room, grabbed my hair and kneed me in the face. A ring of white that smelled of blood rippled through my vision.

'You fucking idiot,' he shouted, before stomping through the hallway to his room.

Roger dashed in from the kitchen where he'd been fixing himself a sandwich.

'Corey,' he said, 'are you okay?'

I heard myself say an underwater yes.

'Let me clean it for you,' he offered.

'No, it's okay, I'll do it myself,' I said, staggering to the bathroom.

I closed the door behind me and examined the damage in the mirror. I washed the blood off my face and was relieved to find my nose hadn't been bent out of shape. Back in my bedroom, I struggled to manage a rising sense of panic when I began thinking about how things could have been worse. What if Liam had kneed the cartilage of my nose into my brain and killed me? What if he'd kept kneeing me in the head and wound up leaving me brain-damaged?

I didn't know what to do. I had a feeling no other foster carers would take me, that foster carers didn't want to take teenagers. Younger children were cuter, less damaged, more likely to be accepted.

I didn't want to provoke Liam again. I agreed with everything he said after that and spent as much time as possible hiding in my room. I never contradicted him and there were no more incidents of violence.

I stopped going to clean Peter's factory. What was the point? A measly fifty dollars for four hours of work.

I was slowly giving up on things.

'Corey,' Melisa said to me over McDonald's as we sat in the park next to the Department's offices one day. 'I have some bad news and some good news.'

'Okay,' I said through a mouthful of cheeseburger.

'The bad news is I'm leaving the Department so I won't be your social worker any more. But there's some good news too: they've accepted you into Nudgee. You're going to get the education you deserve.'

'Oh my God!' I said, nearly choking on my burger. 'Oh my God.' I danced up from the table and leaned over and wrapped her in a hug and she squeezed me back.

I was going to boarding school, where rich people sent their kids. It felt like the universe had extended a hand to me. All I had to do was hold on, climb free of my life and become someone better.

When she dropped me home afterwards, we said goodbye.

'Good luck,' I said to her.

'Good luck to you. Make the most of Nudgee, okay?'

'I promise.'

I waved from the front verandah, feeling like the luckiest kid in the world. I had hope. Life seemed new again. There was a path to a golden place in the future.

I'd claimed the front seat of the car that morning, as we bundled into it for the school drop-off. Liam was running late and emerged from the house a few minutes after the rest of us.

'I want to sit in the front seat,' he demanded, opening my door.

'It's just the front seat,' I said, worried he was going to hit me.

'Get out. I want to sit there.'

'Liam, just get in the back seat,' barked Karen.

He slammed my door and huffily sat down in the seat behind me.

As Karen reversed out of the driveway, Liam berated me.

'You're such an idiot,' he said, voice rising. 'You realise none of us like you, don't you? Nobody would care if you died. You realise that, don't you?'

I edged forward in my seat and pressed myself to the window, worried he was about to punch me in the back of the head.

Liam leaned around my headrest and I flinched. 'I'm not gonna hit you, you moron,' he laughed. 'Nobody's going to care if you fail at Nudgee, which you will you stupid fuckhead.' Satisfied with himself, he sat back and struck up a conversation with his sister Anna.

Nobody in the car intervened or said anything, not even Karen, a silence which the alchemy of my shame turned into an endorsement of Liam's venom. I stayed quiet for the rest of the journey knowing that everything Liam said was true.

Incidents like this had become more frequent in the six months I'd lived with the family. I'd accepted them as inevitable and what I deserved. But news of being accepted into Nudgee had buoyed me, rekindled my instinct for self-protection. Not enough to fight back but enough to flee instead of remaining frozen.

Karen stopped at the school gates. I undid my seatbelt and slid from the car. Liam had already run ahead of me into the grounds. I teared up briefly and disrupted it by gathering the salty liquid at the back of my throat and spitting it on the ground in one big white glob.

I walked over to the area where my group hung out. I didn't feel like being around people, though, so I sat quietly on a bag rack that ran alongside our area.

'Are you all right?' somebody said. I looked up to see my friend Tom.

I started to speak then realised if I did I'd cry. I shook my head mutely.

'What's wrong?' he said in a gentle tone.

I didn't speak for a few seconds. Finally, I explained what had been happening at home.

'Jesus,' said Tom when I'd finished. 'I'm sorry.'

'I won't go back to that house. But I don't have anywhere else to go.'

He was quiet for a few moments. 'You can stay at my house if you want?' he offered.

'Really?'

'I have to ask Mum but I think she'd be fine with it. I'll ring her now.' Tom wandered away to make the call on his mobile and returned a few minutes later. 'She said it's fine. You can stay with us.'

I rang the social worker from the school office, as a school administrator eavesdropped behind the counter while pretending to be absorbed in paperwork. In a low voice, I told the social worker that I wouldn't go back to live with Karen and Roger.

'Are you sure?' the social worker asked, no doubt dreading this new annoyance, another avalanche of paperwork.

'Yes, I'm sure. It's dangerous. Liam's kneed me in the face before, and he's said nobody would care if I die.'

I could tell the social worker was irritated. 'Well,' she said, 'we're going to need to find you a different place now.'

'My friend Tom's mum is happy to take me.'

'Okay. We'll need to do some checks on her. Can you give me Tom's number?'

When the bell rang to signal the end of the school day, I headed to the school office to wait for the social worker. After half an hour I called the Department and a receptionist explained the social worker would be along soon. An hour later nobody had arrived, so I called again only to be given the same explanation.

The sun was going down fast. I worried the Department had forgotten about me.

'I'll have to keep waiting,' I explained to the last lady from the office who was shutting the building up for the day.

I sat on the kerb of the empty car park and waited. At last, car headlights swung over me.

The window rolled down and I saw the social worker. 'Sorry about being late.'

I hopped in the back seat. 'So where am I going?'

She explained that they'd arranged for me to stay the night in a youth shelter nearly an hour's drive away.

When we arrived at the shelter, I got a bad vibe. The social worker handed me off to the youth worker on shift. He showed me to my room, which I'd be sharing with an older boy, Leigh.

'I just got out of juvie,' Leigh bragged. 'I went psycho at a youth worker who tried to touch me.' It wasn't clear what kind of touching it had been. I was open to the possibility somebody had simply placed their hand on his shoulder and been kerbstomped.

I spent the rest of the night agreeing with him. Yes, his DIY tattoos were very cool. Under the harsh bare bulb of our room, he showed me one which was supposed to be a rottweiler. The lines were drawn poorly, however, so features all seemed to fall into one large blob. It looked less like a dog and more like dog shit.

As he sermonised about the best way to survive, I regretted my decision to take a stand against Karen and Roger. I considered calling and asking for them to take me back. I would have done it, except I didn't have the money to make the call from a pay phone.

I lay in bed across the room from Leigh, convinced that he would bludgeon me to death if I fell asleep during his lecture on making a shiv.

———

The social worker rushed through the paperwork and the next day I was able to move in with Tom and his mother, Maggie. After school he and I made the short walk to his house only a few streets away.

I wasn't especially close to Tom and hadn't met his mother. Ascending the stairs to their living room for the first time, I felt nervous.

The house was putrid. The carpet was littered with detritus – lint, plastic, dirty laundry. Two ankle socks strewn in front of the TV remained there for months. The light bulb in the bathroom had blown and remained unchanged, the drain was choked with strands of Maggie's Chewbacca-like hair, and I actually felt *dirtier* after a shower. For the rest of the summer I went as long as I could without showering and I wore socks at all times.

Every day Maggie sat chain-smoking on the couch in a limp white tank top, her gut doughnuting through it, scratching her back with a spatula. I'd sit on the floor a few metres away to avoid the constant plumes of cigarette smoke she emitted.

The mess didn't bother me, though. This was simply the final phase of tribulation before Nudgee, before my golden life.

'You never say hello, Corey. It's very rude,' Maggie said to me one afternoon.

'I'm sorry,' I said, my chest tight. What was going to happen here? This was Helen all over again. Where would I go if she kicked me out? Would this affect my chances of going to Nudgee? 'I'm sorry, I had no idea I was doing wrong.'

'Normal people say hello to one another and sit on the couch and talk, mate.'

Normal people also didn't scratch their back with a spatula, though, so I felt a whole bunch of social norms had been suspended in this house.

I tried to calculate quickly, and knew what I would have to do. This was a necessary stopover, a holding house until Nudgee. The last few years of humiliation in foster homes had evolved into a desire to see myself as better than others, to feel they were beneath me. I'd forgotten that Maggie was a human being who required her ego to be petted, her sense of importance managed.

The next day, I took some of my Youth Allowance money and bought a new shower mat, a black, fluffy rectangle I'd found in a cheap store.

'I bought a shower mat for the house,' I said as I presented it to Maggie on the couch.

'Oh, that's so thoughtful of you, Corey.'

'I noticed we didn't have one so I figured it could help.' I shrugged my shoulders, like a nonchalant saint.

Phew, I thought. I'd appeased her. My place here should be secure until Nudgee.

For the remainder of the summer, upon arriving home from school or a walk, I'd cry out from the bottom of the stairs, 'Hello, Maggie. How was your day?'

'Wonderful, Corey,' she'd yell back. 'How was yours?'

'Awesome,' I replied in my sweetest voice. 'Well,' I'd offer tentatively, 'I'm going to have a nap and then I'll be up in a bit.'

'Okay.'

I'd lie in bed fantasising about Nudgee. I was about to begin my real life. Already I regarded my previous life as far away, in the past. Even my present life had been swallowed up, too. I wasn't here any more; I was somewhere else in a cleaner and truer future.

When I'd finished puffing myself up with the grand scenarios that I was certain Nudgee would entail, I'd trek upstairs and sit in the lounge room and watch mindless afternoon game shows with Maggie and Tom, committing the answers to memory in case I'd need the knowledge at Nudgee.

6

I slept in fits the night before I left for Nudgee. A part of me tried to hold myself back from believing I was going. It felt like there was always a chance the Department could cancel the whole thing at the last minute.

A new social worker I hadn't met yet was picking me up at noon. Since I'd packed everything weeks before, I spent the morning lying on my back in bed as if I were in an opium den, feasting on inner visions. I kept walking to the front door and checking to see if my ride had arrived early.

Finally, there was a knock on the screen door. I bolted to answer it. In the bleaching sunshine stood a blonde woman in a cream blouse and grey trousers.

'Hello,' she said uncertainly. 'My name's Lauren, I'm here to pick up Corey.'

'Oh, hey, I'm Corey.'

'Hi, Corey. Sorry, I can't see you it's so dark in there.' She gave a polite little laugh.

'Who's that?' Maggie grunted from upstairs.

'The social worker,' I yelled.

'All right, I'm coming down.'

When I brought my bags from my room, Maggie and Tom were standing outside with Lauren, Tom in boxers and a white shirt, Maggie in a tired purple terrycloth robe, décolletage like an alligator-skin purse.

I barrelled through the doorway with my luggage and heaved it into the open boot of the car.

'Good luck, mate,' Maggie said, stepping forward for a hug.

I held my breath against her odour, desperate not to vomit. I felt strangely grateful – she was different to other foster carers. She hadn't lashed out, which was more than I could say for Tracey or Helen or Karen.

I found myself unexpectedly earnest. 'Thank you for having me, Maggie.'

I looked at Tom, suddenly mindful of the fact he'd helped me. Noble Tom. His eyes were misty. 'Thanks, Tom,' I said, as he wrapped me in a bear hug.

'You'll do great,' he said, releasing me and placing his hand on my shoulder.

'Okay,' I said. 'We don't want to be late.'

'Yep,' Lauren said, slamming the boot. I walked to the passenger's side of the car, gazed meaningfully at Maggie and Tom, then leaned down and hopped into the passenger's seat, clipping in my seatbelt. Lauren shut her door and looked at me. In a bubbly, celebratory tone she said, 'Are you ready?'

I didn't even know the woman and she was pretending to be excited for me. I played along. 'Hell yeah!'

'Yay!' she cheered, turning the keys in the ignition. The car coughed into a roar and we were away.

I looked back at Tom and Maggie in the rear-view mirror. I knew I'd never see either of them again. I wouldn't need to. I was entering a world of privilege and opportunity now. They were reminders of what I had come from, the last smear of what my life had been before Nudgee. There was no more having to placate Maggie, pretending not to be disgusted by the smoke perennially choking me in the lounge room. I was saying goodbye to the trivial bullshit of foster care. All that would matter at Nudgee were marks. I'd have to study hard, harder than the other boys, but whether or not I succeeded was entirely up to me.

Boarding school. As we drove, I kept repeating the words in my head in lots of three. The words suggested class, dignity, success. Scientists, politicians and businessmen went to boarding schools, and I was following in their footsteps. I was about to become a privately educated boy instead of a foster kid shunted from home to home according to the twin whims of scumbag carers and bureaucrats. I was going to be somebody.

'Okay, this is Nudgee,' Lauren said, guiding the car into the grand entrance. A gigantic Italian Renaissance-style building, golden in the sun, rose up above perfectly manicured lawns dotted with elegant statues. We rounded the redbrick drive, passed the school chapel adorned with baroque stained-glass windows, into the school proper: 136 hectares of state-of-the-art classrooms, a 300-seat auditorium, rugby ovals, athletics track, Olympic-sized pool, gym, basketball and volleyball courts, twelve tennis courts, even a golf course. A high school with a golf course. I stared out the window agog.

We parked out the front of a two-storey brick dormitory. Lauren popped the boot and I retrieved the two red-white-blue bags into which I'd shoved all my worldly possessions. They heaved with every scrap of paper I'd ever written on, all my books, jocks, socks, shorts, shirts, pants and jumpers.

'Want a hand?' Lauren asked.

'I'm okay.' I said it defiantly. I wanted to walk into the dorm independently, with no help.

We came to the front office of the boarding dorm. A fit, greying man in slacks and a blue polo shirt was standing and examining papers on a desk.

He looked up. 'Hi there,' he said in a refined voice. I noticed his chin and nose. They were pointed, aristocratic, the facial structure of some noble Roman general. He was compact, not much taller than me, and looked as if he swam every day and ran on beaches with a golden retriever on a leash.

'I'm Corey.'

'Corey White?'

I deliberately replied 'yes' instead of 'yeah' or 'yep'. I thought it would sound more intelligent.

'I'm Stuart Nolan. And you are?' he asked, extending a hand over the counter to Lauren.

'Just a friend,' I interrupted. 'She's leaving now.'

'Actually, Corey,' she said in the soft, controlled voice of a social worker, 'I'll need to chat with Stuart.' I shrank, embarrassed. I'd hoped

I wouldn't need to introduce anyone at Nudgee to the social worker. 'Hi Stuart, I'm Lauren. I'm from the Department of Family Services.'

'Ah. I read that Corey's a foster kid.'

'Yes. We just need to go over a few things.'

I eyeballed the corridor near the office and was relieved nobody else was around. Maybe the contaminating information could be contained.

After several minutes of Lauren giving Department contact details to Mr Nolan, it was over. 'Would you like to see your room?' asked Mr Nolan.

'Yes,' I said. 'Okay, bye, Lauren. Thanks.' I jerked my head at her to indicate she should leave. She took the hint and said goodbye as Mr Nolan led me to my room.

We made our way down a long hallway stretching roughly fifty metres. On each side there were curtained doorways, beyond which each room was subdivided into six smaller sections, each containing a bed, cupboard, desk and chair. As we walked, Mr Nolan informed me this was one of four such wings in the residence, so that the dorm held maybe a hundred boys.

'I'm the dorm master,' he continued, 'along with my wife, Mrs Nolan, who you'll meet later. If you need anything, please don't hesitate to ask.'

'Excellent,' I said, like a Shakespearean actor.

We entered a doorway, walking past the first two nooks to mine, in the middle section.

'This will be your room,' Mr Nolan said to his clipboard. Glancing up at me, he smiled. 'I'll let you unpack and settle in.'

'Thank you,' I said in my least foster-kid voice.

'We'll have a barbecue at 3 p.m. for new boarders on the lawn. I'll see you then.'

I bowed my head slightly. 'Splendid.'

I packed my things away in the cupboard, made my bed and sat at my desk in a pleasant trance, listening to the din of boys arriving to their rooms all along the wing, mothers and fathers planting kisses and securing promises of phone calls.

I was in boarding school now.

'Barbecue!' boomed an unseen man a little later, tearing me from my reverie. 'Barbecue!'

Outside, on lush grass beneath a tree, Mr Nolan was cooking sausages and onions on a gleaming barbecue. Beside it was a table on which rested mountains of plates, bread and condiments. A group of perhaps thirty boys milled around. We introduced ourselves shyly.

When someone asked what my parents did, I lied and said they were in 'business'.

'Wow,' said Claudio, a shiny-cheeked Italian kid. 'My dad's in imports-exports. What does your dad do?'

'I'm not actually sure.' They seemed to buy it.

The next morning, old boarders filed into the dorms in snaking caravans of parents and suitcases. We watched them from the safety of the foosball table in the kitchen area, saw the high-fives, playful teasing about haircuts, headlocks, nipple cripples and wet willies. The returning boarders glanced over at us new boys flocked together like sheep. Most looked away indifferently. A few came and introduced themselves in a hurricane of handshakes and names soon forgotten.

I felt a chasm between the groups. Old boys had already formed their friendship circles so I figured it would be a waste of time to even attempt to crack into them. It was just like foster care: ties had already been formed, broken and re-formed. Neural pathways, intangible bindings. There was no point expelling energy trying to belong to them. Their history was too great an impediment.

Initially, I was taken aback by the rough and tumble of the dorms. I'd expected boys wearing monocles fetching watches on gold chains to check the time. Reality varied. Zero of my fellow boarders satirised the poetry of T. S. Eliot. Instead they black-bagged one another with fart-filled pillowcases or shaved each other's eyebrows in titanic struggles of seven boys on one.

Nudgee was an elite private school, but more important than that, it was a rugby school. Intellectual pursuits were viewed with suspicion, as signals of a defect that could rupture the camaraderie and togetherness. We play footy. We are Nudgee boys. Thinking would only threaten that.

During an afternoon studying in my room, Sam Bridge stuck his head in to measure my heresy.

'Studying, are ya?' he asked.

'Yep.'

'Ya studying a cock, are ya?'

'Yep.'

'A huge big cock ya wanna suck?'

'Yep.'

'Sounds pretty gay.'

'Yep.'

'All right, enjoy the gay cock.'

'Will do.'

And back I went to my religious studies essay on Mahayana Buddhism.

'Oi, Corey.' Sam Bridge was back.

'Yep?'

'Sorry for being dumb,' he said earnestly. 'Seriously, can you help me with an essay later?'

I peered up from my desk, weighing the benefits of being on the good side of this barbarian. If I helped, he'd probably give me peace in the future.

'Sure thing,' I said.

'Great,' he said, sitting on my bed. 'I have no idea what to write for it. Because it's about gay cocks!' He cackled and skipped out of the room, howling away down the corridor. 'Gay cock!' he roared.

'Gay cock!' someone else yelled.

I couldn't help but chuckle.

One term I played rugby but I was called out for my strange running style. Apparently I ran like a chicken.

It didn't help that I had never played rugby union in my life. I'd grown up playing rugby league, not union, and, while there was some basic crossover in rules, I didn't know the intricacies. I barely knew what was happening in the games. That combined with my hearing difficulty meant I spent a lot of time on the wing, terrified of being passed the ball.

Rugby union was also far more vicious than league. I learned about the practice of 'rucking': when somebody was tackled, players on the opposing team would gleefully try to trample him and slash his skin open with the spikes of their boots.

Huddled together on the sidelines before one match, our captain concluded a psych-up speech by commanding us to 'ruck the shit out of these fucks'.

My teammates roared savagely but I fretted. All I could see happening was that we would ruck them hard then they would ruck us harder, and so it would go on escalating. Knowing my luck, I'd be the guy who copped the nuclear bomb at the end of this and somebody would probably ruck my face off. I'd be made faceless from a game I didn't even like or understand. Couldn't my teammates see we were starting an arms race? But I didn't want to be seen as a coward so I remained silent, like a coward.

Food was a common boarding-school gripe but I struggled to comprehend why. I was in heaven.

For breakfast there was the most fantastic smorgasbord: scrambled eggs, hash browns, fried tomatoes, mushrooms, cereals, yoghurt, fruit salad, white and wholemeal toast. For morning tea, gigantic biscuits, bananas, apples and mandarins.

Lunch times were usually cold meat sandwiches, a few slices of chicken loaf or ham stuffed into a bread roll the size of my hand, finished off with tomato, barbecue or honey mustard sauce. Afternoon tea saw more fruit. Dinners were a rotating roster of steak, chicken, fish, steamed vegetables, shepherd's pie, stir-fry and lasagne.

It was the best eating I'd ever done.

In the first few weeks at Nudgee, I used to wander around the grounds once school had finished. Its wealth staggered me, the feeling of possibility. It felt like an intellectual Xanadu. I spent hours reading in the school library. I read Hemingway, Kafka, Faulkner, McCullers. I read Aristotle, Socrates, Plato, Descartes, Schopenhauer, Kierkegaard, Russell, Camus. I tried and failed to read Wittgenstein.

I was awestruck by the most concentrated and dazzling array of human thought. My life was rich with the epiphanic.

Until that point the only books I'd read were Little Golden Books, the Bible, Goosebumps and a series of erotic vampire horror novels that I'd used to masturbate at Tracey's.

Despite this opening of my intellectual world, I was finding the discipline required at Nudgee difficult. Every night we were assigned several hours of homework for each subject, which we were to manage concurrently with longer assessment pieces.

I had so much to learn and unlearn, and I had the time management skills of a narcoleptic in a hammock. It took everything I had, took staying up well past midnight and waking early, to keep going. I flogged myself, driven by a fear of returning to foster care. Anything but that.

———

Each Sunday all boarders were required to attend 6 p.m. Mass in the school chapel. It was my first encounter with anything approaching a ritual. I thought it was nonsense. The priests ran through the motions, delivering insipid sermons I was sure they had ripped off the internet.

The first time I attended, I had no idea of the process. Like a character in a Chaplin film, I kept kneeling at the wrong time or standing up too soon, every mistake rippling through me.

Despite clearly not being a Catholic, I took communion because, to my mind, it helped me keep secret the fact I was a foster kid. Any boys who wondered why I never called my parents or received visits from family, upon seeing me bob up and down like a broken whack-a-mole, would think, 'I was beginning to suspect White's legal guardian is the State, but seeing him Mr Magoo his way through Mass has convinced me he's just a good Catholic boy with a proper intact family, nervous in the House of the Lord.'

As I drank the communion wine I always promised the God I didn't believe in that this time would be the last time.

Josh and Steven started bullying me. It began softly. Seeing my devotion to chess, they coined the clever nickname Chess Boy. It spread around the dorms and, as if by some eldritch magic, all trace of my name Corey disappeared. I'd be sitting in the toilet and if someone knocked on the door and I answered, they'd say, 'Chess Boy.' Not as a question, or even an urging for me to hurry. Just a statement. *Chess Boy*. Like a child calling the moon the moon.

A few weeks later, Steven spread a rumour that he'd caught me masturbating over my chessboard. I didn't bother to contest the charges.

Another time I returned from Sunday lunch to find condoms arranged like a minefield in my bed.

'Who the fuck did this?' I yelled. I could hear Steven squawking in his room. 'Who the fuck put condoms in my bed?' I looked more closely. They were filled with a creamy white substance. 'Is this cum?' I shouted. 'Are these condoms full of fucking cum?' Panoramic laughter filled the wing.

Steven pushed through the curtain. 'What's the matter, Corey?' he asked with false sympathy.

'Did you do this?'

A smirk flashed across his fat head. 'Did I do what?'

'Did you put cum-filled condoms in my bed?'

He smirked. 'No! Who has that much cum?'

This had to have been the work of a group. A red mist overtook me as I imagined the wing co-ordinating jerking off, setting sentries, taking shifts. But maybe it wasn't cum. I picked up one of the condoms. It wasn't tied.

'What are you doing?' Steven asked shrilly.

I put the condom opening to my nostril and sniffed.

'What the fuck?' Steven stuttered. 'Oh my gawd! Corey's sniffing the condoms!'

'It's shampoo,' I protested to where Steven had been standing.

He was out in the hallway now. 'Oh my gawd, Chess Boy sniffed the condoms. He's a cum sniffer!'

I followed him out, still holding the condom. 'It wasn't cum!' I said, shaking it at him.

It was too late. No matter how many times I asserted that it wasn't cum in the condoms, Cum Sniffer was added to the list of my nicknames.

Once or twice a term, we boarded a bus on a Friday night and attended a dance with an all-girls boarding school. One evening we jetted off to boogie with the girls from All Hallows.

The bus pulled up and Mr Fleming, the Boarding Events Co-ordinator, stood up.

'Okay, boys,' he bellowed. 'Best behaviour. No shenanigans. Treat the girls with respect and dignity.'

Somebody yelled back, 'It's pussy time!' and Mr Fleming shook his head and got off the bus.

Pussy-related utterances echoed through the bus.

'Pusssssyyyy,' said Albino Adam, hanging from two poles like a milky orangutan.

'Time to feed the kitties some meat.'

A boy nicknamed Wombat yelled, 'We're getting cunt!'

'Yeah the bois!' someone sang.

'Boyyy!'

'Pussy for the bois!'

Eager to fit in, I offered a line. Clearing my throat, sweaty palms, I shouted, 'Yeah, the girls!' Nobody noticed that I'd even spoken. I shut my mouth and filed out awkwardly.

Outside, as we walked through the school grounds, I lingered behind Steven and Josh, uncertain if I was welcome or not.

I began to panic about what I would do inside the dance hall. I had no real social group. I prayed that a girl would take a liking to me just so I didn't have to wander alone. I didn't care whether we kissed or ground our hips together. I just wanted cover for my own complete lack of friends.

Inside, on the other side of the hall, were the girls, visions of perfection. We regarded them with awkward carnality and everyone's theatrical bragging died in their mouths. Boys adjusted their crotch to make sure their erections weren't visible to the girls or each other.

Hip-hop music began throbbing throughout the hall. Boys ventured out into the space, slowly merging with the girls.

I looked at a girl and moved towards her. We danced facing each other, locking eyes. I could feel the heat of the room. She was cute. She gazed into my eyes and I gazed into her eyes. She spun around on the spot, her dress a brief hovering disc. We made eye contact again as she unscrewed her water bottle and took a large seductive sip.

Pounding with lust, terrified of rejection, I moved closer. I reached out and placed my hands on her hips and swayed with her. She swayed back. *Here we go*, I thought. We danced awhile, our hands placed rigidly on each other's hips. I could feel my erection bulging. I'd arranged my penis vertically beneath the top of my underwear as a strategy to hide it and I prayed it wouldn't boing out.

The girl turned around and kept dancing. I shuffled close behind her. Momentarily, I felt dizzy from the strawberry scent of her hair. Suddenly I felt her body stiffen, saw her turn around with an angry look on her face. I stepped back, confused. A moment later I felt something strike my head, and my eyes flashed white.

I wasn't sure what had happened until I heard Josh yell. Despite the clamour of the dance floor, despite 'Sandstorm' blaring, it was clear. 'Chess Boy got bottled!'

So that was what had happened. My lady dancing companion had flogged my head with her water bottle.

Josh was bent double with laughter, pointing at me.

Steven came over, lifting Josh up by his elbows. 'What happened?' he shouted. 'Tell me!' Steven was so eager he'd left the girl he'd been pashing for thirty minutes standing right where she was, lips puckered and eyes closed.

Catching his breath, Josh panted, 'Corey . . . tried to get behind . . . that girl . . . and dance . . . She turned around . . . and bottled him.'

'What?'

'She got her water bottle . . . and belted him. On his face.'

Steven hooted and slapped his thighs. 'Oh my gawwwd,' he moaned, quivering with schadenfreude.

Word spread. I, Chess Boy, had been bottled.

I sat down in a chair on the fringe of the heaving mass of dancing and pashing boys and girls. I didn't have the heart to dance any more, even after an emissary of my assailant came and apologised on her behalf. My microscopic teenage confidence had been annihilated in an act of pretty funny violence.

On the bus back to school, the consensus was the Bottler had overreacted, but it was cold comfort. I felt it was not a just bottling. 'I don't understand, I wasn't being a dickhead. I was trying to be a gentleman!'

'Oh, she was crazy,' Steven said. 'You'd been dancing with her too! She must have been sickened by your sweat and –' he acted out The Bottling.

Josh chipped in with an alternative theory. 'She was like a horse. You shouldn't have approached from behind.'

For the rest of term, whenever I returned to my room from school or showering, I'd find a water bottle on my desk or placed on my pillow.

During rugby season, we made our way to Ross Oval for Spirit Practice once a week. We squeezed into the old grandstand while the Spirit Committee led war cries in rehearsal for the games we had to attend on weekends.

'N!' they'd yell.

'N!' we'd echo, going back and forth to spell out Nudgee.

The main school war cry was the baroque

Hokitika Hokitika Whish Bang Whop
Ingo Buddy Buddy Give It to Them Hot
Paw the Boot Paw the Boot Tackle Hard and True
Nudgee, Nudgee Blue White Blue
Yah Yah Ingo Yah
Ingo Popego Tarrawerah Wopego
Yah Boska

hollered at a breakneck pace. I always flubbed the words and ended up simply howling in a monotone until it was over.

Spirit Practice was an exquisite scene: nerds and social outcasts shouting war cries of brotherhood alongside boys who bullied them the rest of the time. The intimidation influenced the rehearsal too: if those lower in the social hierarchy didn't yell passionately enough, a more athletic boy was liable to give them a stabbing look of menace or jab them in the back and rebuke them. In Soviet Russia under Stalin, people would applaud his speeches for up to an hour, their hands hot and raw, because everyone was terrified of stopping first and being seen as disloyal. The dynamic of Spirit Practice was not dissimilar.

The volume of our screaming gradually rose over the course of the lunch break, nobody wanting to attract attention for not being sufficiently zealous. As the frenzy built, you had to raise your voice even further to make sure you weren't seen to be lagging. Then everybody else did the same. So you yelled even louder, half-wondering if it was possible to yell your eyes clean out of your head. Afterwards, as we trudged back to class, we croaked in pain from our fervour.

The whole thing felt hollow and absurd, since I'd witnessed the underbelly of this 'brotherhood'.

One boy in my Legal Studies classes, Chesterton, a porcine communist who shoehorned Marx into every conversation he could, was regularly told to fuck off and die. He'd do nothing but unzip his pencil case and someone would growl, 'Die, you fat cunt.'

There were dozens of punching bags like Chesterton and each time they were pushed against a wall or humiliated needlessly, it ate away at my belief in our supposedly noble fraternity. At sixteen I'd discovered the first pleasure and last refuge of people who feel like outsiders: identifying hypocrisy and feeling clever for it, while doing nothing to remedy it.

Sean Hare was the bleakest counter example. The kindest thing you could say of Hare was that he was having a difficult puberty. His face was a mash of pimples and he stank. I once heard somebody yell at him, 'Your face is wrong.' Someone told me that in Year 8 a group of boarders had locked him in a cupboard and poured talcum powder through a hole in the top, taunting him as he coughed to death. Only the intervention of a teacher saved his life. They opened the door and Hare tumbled out, a pure white creature gasping for air.

In the hallways now, years later, boys punched him in the stomach, slapped him over the head and told him to shower. His 'brothers' turned on him like jackals.

Their sadism repulsed me but what sickened me more was Hare's reaction. Rather than distancing himself from the cruel bozos, he'd spent years toadying up to them to try to win their affection. At Spirit Practice, Hare was the most passionate of us all.

It only occurs to me now that Hare was doing what I had done to survive foster care: twisting to the whims of his tormentors, hoping that by making himself a more satisfyingly pathetic creature he might minimise his suffering, like someone campaigning to be the front of a human centipede. If you must be in a human centipede, better there than at the back or, God forbid, the middle.

Cacophony woke me. Somebody said, 'Fucking disgusting, fucking disgusting.' I got out of bed and popped my head into the hallways to see dozens of boys massed in a communion of outrage.

'What's happening?' I asked Willis, a cricket-obsessed boy from close to where I was born.

'Isiah has been taking photos of my fucking feet,' spat Willis.

I laughed. 'What?'

'Ask someone else,' he said and stormed off.

'What's happening?' I asked Ryan Morrison, a weightlifter red as a sausage and shaped like one too.

'Isiah was photographing people's feet while they were asleep,' he chuckled, taking a large gulp of his protein shake.

That morning, Isiah had gone for a shower and left his cupboard unlocked. His roommate David had gone to play a practical joke on him only to discover that the inside of Isiah's wardrobe was plastered with photos of feet. Worse, among the dozens of photographs blu-tacked in the cupboard, David had recognised the glossy reproductions of his very own feet. Within minutes, everyone in the dorm knew and three other boys, including Willis, had identified their feet, pointing in outrage between their toes and the images of their toes, correlating complexions, hairs, bunions and scars. A few feet remained unidentified, presumably from shame on the part of their owners.

Without looking, I knew that Isiah hadn't taken photos of my feet. I wasn't flattering myself. At best my feet were a 2.

I asked where Isiah was and was told that he was gone. Apparently he had toddled back into the wing from a relaxing shower, towel around his waist, squeaking down the hallway in his wet thongs. He saw the crowd and had immediately realised the jig was up. Panicked by his newfound status as a pariah, he'd turned around and fled the dorms via a fire escape, legging it up to the school office to call his parents.

I couldn't understand the impulse. Feet had all the erotic appeal of picking up dog shit.

Mr Nolan called a boarders' assembly that afternoon in a classroom across the road from our dorms.

'Now, as some of you may know, there's been an incident regarding the photographing of feet.' In an ashen-faced speech, Mr Nolan repeatedly referenced 'the photographing of people's feet' to widespread snickering.

'The boy in question has returned home while the school decides what to do. If anybody would like counselling, it is available.'

Nelson piped up. 'Mr Nolan, I think I need to see a counsellor.'

'Yes?'

'I can't deal with the fact Isiah *didn't* take photos of my feet. I feel unbeautiful.'

The room exploded in hooting and hollering.

'If that's true,' replied Mr Nolan, suppressing a smile, 'by all means approach myself or any member of staff for assistance. If that's true.'

The reaction seemed overblown to me, but emotion was high.

'It's not really the badness of photographing feet that people mind,' Claudio sermonised after dinner later that night. 'It's the creepiness. While people sleep. Not something Nudgee Boys should do to each other.'

'True,' agreed Mark Day.

'It's pretty sick,' offered Neil James, taking a bite of his post-dinner banana.

Isiah returned to the dorms two weeks later. In the interim, extravagant theories proliferated. He'd been selling the photos to foot-fetish websites. Former friends, who knew his parents sold photography equipment in Papua New Guinea, speculated they were in on the whole thing.

Nevertheless, he returned, bravely I thought, withdrawn and shrunken. Nobody talked to him for a few days but within a month his old friends joined him where he sat alone at dinner, even David, who'd found the photos of his own feet and sparked the exile. In time, the incident was forgotten.

In truth, I was quietly pleased about the whole affair. Isiah had always been terrible to me. He'd never been short of a snide comment or an unfriendly push in the back waiting in line for dinner. When he returned from exile, he was much kinder. One less person whose ego and thirst for power I had to fret about. And he didn't bother me for months, until later in the year he paid me out for something or other. Shocked that he'd violated a new unspoken treaty, I turned to him at the table and said, 'Why don't you go photograph someone's feet, you fucking foot faggot.'

He stared gobsmacked at his toast then got up and left. I kept eating my breakfast, a hot ball of anger scalding my throat. I regretted lashing out, but I didn't need another shithead to deal with.

For all its faults, I loved Nudgee. I can imagine another person being genuinely upset by all that went on, but I shrugged it off. After foster care, it was water off a duck's back. It wasn't like I cried myself to sleep. A lot of the time, it was hilarious. Seeing a boy running down the hallways because someone had stolen his towel while he was showering was just funny. Boys being waterbombed as they slept was comedy gold.

And boarding school life suited me. The loveless egalitarianism of it. While the dorm wasn't a family, it also wasn't foster care. There was no affection given to others and not you. You didn't need to appease a carer to ensure your place. I wished I'd been in boarding school all my life.

The routine was appealing too. We were woken by our house mother at 7.30 a.m. Everybody was to be out of bed by 8 a.m. at the latest. We showered, walked up into the school to eat breakfast, returned to the dorms to brush our teeth, then headed off to school.

In the afternoons, we went swimming in the school pool. Racing each other, holding competitions to see who could hold their breath the longest. In the evenings, we played foosball downstairs or table tennis upstairs.

On Saturdays, we slept in until 10 a.m. and then went to play sports or supported Nudgee teams if they were playing home games. Sundays were lazy affairs. Boys gathered around computers in their rooms to watch movies or TV shows. That was the easy rhythm of our lives week in and week out.

For the first time in my life, I had a group of friends in school I hung out with because I liked them, not because I didn't want to be alone. We went to breakfast together in the morning, sat with each other during morning tea, lunch and afternoon tea, and went to dinner in a group. I didn't tell any of them that I was a foster kid, so I felt there was always a dishonest foundation to our relationships, but, weighing the disadvantages, lying by omission felt the safest route.

The sole aspect of Nudgee that involved disclosing I was a foster kid were my visits to the Student Equity Office and its staff members, Jane and Brother Michael.

Jane was a lay staff member, but Brother Michael was a Christian Brother. He had a torturously unexpressive face. Whenever I spoke to him, I always projected my worst fear onto his blankness. I'd find myself thinking things like, *He despises my criminogenic head. I bet he prays to God for my death or quadriplegia.*

From the outset, I was aware of the power Jane and Brother Michael had over me, that they could expose me as a foster kid at any moment, and I tried to stay away from the office as much as possible.

As the end of my first term at Nudgee drew closer, the question arose as to where I'd live during break. Jane had told me that the boarding school would be closed and no exception could be made for me to stay on.

I hadn't heard anything from the Department until Mr Nolan appeared in my room after school one afternoon as I was solving chess puzzles at my desk.

'Corey, Sachin is here to see you.'

'Sachin?'

'Sachin.'

I walked into the hallway and was greeted by a bearded Indian man. 'Hello, Corey,' he said in a thick accent.

'Hi,' I replied, unsure of who he was.

'I'm Sachin, from the Department.'

My chest became a garden of fear. Were they pulling me out of Nudgee?

'What do you want?' I asked.

'I'm your new social worker.'

I inspected him properly. He wore crisp slacks and an impeccable red gingham shirt. His beard was so neatly groomed it could have been a wig. His arms were crossed tightly and he was emanating an intense awkward air.

'Let's go,' I whispered, angry that he'd come into the dorms. Someone else might find out I was a foster kid. 'Thanks, Mr Nolan,' I said, pressing past and leading Sachin downstairs and out of the building. He jogged to catch up with me.

'What's up?' I asked, directing him away to the empty lawns.

'I want to take you to Clyde House.'

'What's Clyde House?'

'Clyde House is where the Department wants you to stay when you're not at Nudgee.'

'Okay, sounds good.'

'We need you to visit there.'

'Well, it doesn't matter what I think, does it? Just set it up and I'll go there.'

He shook his head. 'It would be good for you, Corey.'

'Do I absolutely have to do it?'

'Yes, yes. Please.'

'Fine. Well, let me know when you want me to go check the place out.'

'This afternoon,' he said.

'Now?'

'Yes.'

'Jesus Christ. You couldn't have given me more notice? I've got a lot of work due.'

'I am sorry but you must see the place today.'

'Fine. Let's go.'

We made a beeline for Sachin's Department-issued silver sedan and got in. Wending through the afternoon traffic, I thought about how inept he was. A lifetime in foster care meant I knew he'd dropped the ball today. He should have called instead of dropping in unannounced. Where did they get these buffoons from?

Suddenly we screeched to a halt and I was thrown forward, my head almost slamming the dashboard. I looked up to see a ute diagonal to us. A man leaned out the window and screamed, 'Oi, fuckhead! Watch where you're going!'

Sachin scrabbled in his door, then in the console between our seats, and the window slid closed. But in the chaos, he'd taken his foot off the brake, and the car rolled forward towards the man in the ute. His eyes widened in anger and through the window I heard him yelling, 'What the fuck are you doing? Are you slow?' Sachin whimpered and slammed on the brakes again. 'You dumb cunt!' screamed the man, resembling for a moment a half-human, half-car enraged ute-centaur.

Sachin wove the car around the screaming ute creature and we drove off.

I was frozen stiff, my arse numb from terror. 'Do you even know how to drive?' I said.

'Yes, I do,' Sachin said.

'I don't feel comfortable in this car, man.'

'We must go to Clyde House.'

I saw Sachin's hands were trembling, but I felt no sympathy.

For the rest of the drive, I watched him out of the corner of my eye, ready to take the steering wheel should he decide to start clapping for fun or eating a sandwich. He ran a few red lights but we survived and, after half an hour of Sachin fiddling with the GPS and driving down the wrong streets, we finally pulled into the driveway of Clyde House.

It was nice enough. A single-storey brick house with a freshly mown front lawn dotted with pine trees, and a basketball hoop above the driveway. Sachin honked the car horn, possibly accidentally.

A large, friendly woman came out to meet us. 'Hello, hello! I'm Eileen!' She seemed about fifty, in jeans and sneakers with a white shirt and glasses. We introduced ourselves and she beckoned for us to follow her inside.

Stepping through the doorway, I was surprised the place didn't smell. It seemed clean, if sparsely furnished. Two simple blue couches angled at a television in one corner, a kitchen table in another. White tiles ran throughout the house.

'I should give you the tour then.' She fetched a set of keys from her pocket and opened a door to the right of us. 'This is the office for the social workers,' she said, swinging it open. A blast of cool air rose up to greet us.

'Buzz!' she snapped before I'd even had a chance to look in. I jostled beside her and saw a rotund man in a faded red shirt sitting at a table munching a sandwich. 'What are you doing in here?'

Through a mouthful of bread and egg, he explained. 'Sorry, darl, I was just having my sandwich in the air conditioning.'

'You're not supposed to eat in here. We'll talk later,' she warned, shutting the door and turning to us. 'That's my husband, Buzz.'

'Yes,' said Sachin.

'Let's go have a look at your room.' We walked past the lounge area and into a small hallway. 'There are four rooms here, but two of them are empty at the moment. This one's yours.'

It was small with freshly painted white walls, blue carpet and a single bed. Apart from a chest of drawers in the corner, the room was bare. It had a neutral smell and I couldn't see any cockroaches.

'It's nothing special but it's clean and quiet,' said Eileen.

'It's good,' I replied.

Over orange juice and biscuits at the dining table she explained the house rules. 'We're not too strict here, but we don't allow drugs, alcohol or anybody in your room apart from you. All sex must take place off the property.' She laughed, I smiled and Sachin nodded, not understanding the joke.

'What about food?' I asked.

'Breakfast, lunch and dinner are served. You can make snacks outside of those times but you'll need to get permission from workers if you want to use cutlery, especially knives. We've had incidents.'

'Okay.'

'No knives?' asked Sachin, pressing his pen to a clipboard.

'Yes, no knives,' confirmed Eileen.

'No knives,' repeated Sachin, making a note.

'Think of it as a mini-orphanage, but better,' Eileen chortled, as she saw us off at the door.

On the way home to Nudgee, Sachin asked whether I'd like to live at Clyde House.

'Do I really have a choice?'

'No,' he said bluntly, curled over the steering wheel in fierce concentration.

I liked Eileen, though I knew sociopaths always give good first impressions. The test would be when I was just one-on-one with her, when nobody from the Government was there monitoring her potential malice. Her husband Buzz seemed a harmless enough guy, like a hapless man in a dishwashing liquid commercial, but you could never tell. And Eileen had also mentioned that she and Buzz were not always there. Residential workers came in for 24-hour to 48-hour shifts on weekends and sometimes during the week. What would they be like? I had my reservations and concerns but I was powerless. I was going to Clyde House regardless of what I thought.

On the way back, Sachin only nearly crashed twice.

I had mostly stuck to philosophy during my expeditions in the school library, steering clear of fiction. I preferred the moral of stories over the stories themselves. I wanted to know the essence of things. And then I found a ninety-page novella called *Metamorphosis* by Franz Kafka, about a man named Gregor Samsa who wakes up as a giant cockroach in his bed. His family, whom he supports financially by working as a travelling salesman, disowns him upon discovering his hideous transformation. He remains in the room for months. Only his sister feeds him. Eventually she stops and he begins to starve. Realising he must flee to survive, he attempts to escape only for his father to throw an apple at him, which lodges in his back, mortally wounding him.

He retreats back into his by-now filthy room and prepares to die. In his final moments, Kafka writes, 'Gregor Samsa looked back on his family with love and devotion.'

When I read that sentence, a volcano of tears erupted from me.

Here was a story that felt real. There was no happy ending: a good man died at the end, and that felt authentic. It seemed to strike at the heart of being alive.

Gregor Samsa was Christ-like, loving in the face of enmity and neglect. But he was more than Christ-like. Christians spoke of Jesus sacrificing his life for humanity's sins, but he was a god. Gregor was no god. No divine blood flowed through his veins. He was a human. Well, a human mind inside a cockroach. When he thought of his family with love, he did it believing in nothing but an abyss after death, fulfilling no prophecy. He simply died loving those who had wronged him. The vastness of this filled me with awe and reverence. It was easy for Jesus to cop a crucifixion, but little old Gregor was a fucking fabric salesman.

The pity I felt for him spread osmotically to me. I felt sorrier for myself as time went on. I felt so up against everything. I'd think of foster care, of having to go to Clyde House, of my shattered family, how nobody cared if I lived or died. It was a pretty depressing thought. Even if I did graduate from Nudgee, even if I went to university, what then? Go to university where I'd face more challenges? Even if I graduated from university, what then? Go do a job where I'd face more challenges? Even if I did get a job, what then? I would still be alone. Because I knew deep down, with every fleck of my being, that I was rotten and doomed. I'd been born with an apple in my back. How long would I live with it festering there?

———

Pushing myself to study as hard as possible, I excelled at English, Study of Religion, Geography, Legal Studies and Biology. Maths was far tougher, though. In my first term, I failed.

I snuck to the Equity office, making sure no student had seen me, and knocked on Jane's door.

She looked up. 'Hello, Corey. What brings you here?'

I showed her the report card while trying not to cry. 'What happens if I fail again?'

Jane was grave. 'You may lose your scholarship.'

My vision glistened.

'We'll get you a maths tutor.'

Brother Michael and Jane had insisted on me joining in the life of the school, but my failure in maths put an end to that. I felt angry at them. I could lose Nudgee. What good would *socialising* be then? They weren't the ones who faced returning to suburbs of grinding insecurity without family or support. Back to foster care. To the horrible nothingness.

I felt deceived by their injunctions to have fun, make friends, enjoy life. They were either stupid or didn't care about me. As I sat there boiling in my anger, I promised myself to not trust anyone at this school again. From that moment, I sacrificed everything for good grades. Nothing else mattered.

I stopped going to meals with my friends, either having toast in the dorms or creeping into the kitchen at the last possible minute and grabbing food to go. I read my mathematics textbook on the toilet. I drifted away from everyone. What choice did I have? If I failed maths again, I might not even be at Nudgee to drift away from them.

My sole social outlet was chess. Every lunch time I'd go to the French classroom which functioned as the chess club. Since lunch was only about a half an hour, I'd figured it wasn't long enough to do any proper study so chess seemed an appropriate leisure activity.

By third term I could count the people I was friendly with on a bomb disposalist's hand.

After finishing my final exam for the year, I packed up my room and called Clyde House to be picked up. Buzz came in a white people mover van which I was ashamed to be seen in.

'Ready for a holiday?' he asked.

'I've got a lot of reading to do over the holidays,' I said. 'I need to read all of Shakespeare's plays.'

'Sounds like fun,' he said.

Christmas came and passed, New Year's too. I read constantly, desperate to catch up after years of lacklustre schooling.

Throughout the summer, Eileen and other workers would ask if I wanted to come on some inane trip to the beach or mountains.

'Sorry, I'm reading a book,' I'd say, closing the door. I didn't have time to gallivant around in nature. I was behind and excursions were a waste of time.

Eileen pressed on through the wooden door. 'Corey, you need fresh air. This isn't healthy for you.'

'I don't have time for health! I have more important things to think about.'

I read the plays of Camus, his novels too. *The Picture of Dorian Gray*. I tried to read Shakespeare's plays but the language was too difficult for me to follow and I gave up.

My only genuine recreation time was masturbating: five or six times a day I'd allow myself a twenty-minute break to let off steam by masturbating like Ted Bundy on Viagra. After I flushed the tissues down the toilet, I'd get straight back to whatever I was doing.

When my eyes tired and couldn't focus on the words, or I just couldn't stomach the thought of doing any more damn reading, I'd fall back on my bed and marinate in self-disgust. Why couldn't I concentrate for longer periods? Why was I so weak, so pathetic? I wished I was a perfect and tireless machine, and all the frailty and slowness in me could be extinguished.

7

Teachers told us that Year 12 would make earlier years seem like a walk in the park.

They were right.

Our homework tripled. The textbooks were heavier, with tinier fonts, more information.

The heavy workload shredded the hours. I quit playing chess altogether. I barely socialised, a hermit in the midst of a hundred people. People, when they spoke to me, now called me Corey; the playful teasing nicknames had fallen by the wayside.

We'd moved to a new dorm with a new dorm master, Mr Hughes, who resembled a Guess Who character. A snowy-haired, round-faced man, he was beloved by many of us for his gentleness and willingness to treat us like adults. Unfortunately, his discipline left something to be desired.

Study time in the dorms was a joke. Boys played games of hallway cricket or passed a football. 50 Cent's 'Candy Shop' blared from

Felix Wang's radio. There was a feral energy in the dorms which made study impossible.

It infuriated me. These rich bastards didn't have to do well in school. They could always be parachuted into a plum job at Daddy's law firm. I, on the other hand, needed good marks. I had the DNA of a criminal. I drew my curtain and seethed.

News had spread of Donald Jameson's giant balls and the tragic tale of how they'd come to be so huge. Donald had been sitting on a port rack one lunch time chatting with friends when the bell had rung for class. Poor, piteous Donald had gone to leap off the port rack but, somehow, his testicles had become caught in the gap between slats. He'd hung briefly, a horizontal Christ, attached to wood by his ballsack. A gigantic popping sound had launched him into a new level of pain and he'd belly-flopped onto the concrete, scrotum fluid and blood trickling down his legs as he screamed. He had obviously not been wearing underwear, though he later insisted that he'd been wearing boxer shorts.

'How big were your balls before?' someone ventured.

'Not as big as they are now,' grimaced Donald, enjoying the awed reactions to surviving such a horror.

For the next few weeks, we all relished seeing Donald's giant swollen scrotum, horrified by the indigo disfigurement. He'd flop his injury out at the merest hint of a request and in the mornings, as he hobbled down the hallway after showering, you could see the monstrous bulge in his towel.

One Saturday night, Nelson darted up to Donald in a kitchenette as he was making toast and slapped Donald's bloated nuts. Right out of the blue, for no reason other than he thought it would be funny. This was the humour I'd become used to, but with the barbarism turned up several notches.

Nelson was on one side of a division in the dorms, between those who were going to university and the VET students doing vocational courses. Boarders in the academic stream had to knuckle down while, for those in the VET strand of subjects, it was just another year. Their subjects were not nearly as difficult, and a lot of their work could only be done at school anyway, so homework was minimal.

It was a split and its effects were widening. It felt as though things had become harder, nastier.

The only thing that bothered me about it, though, was the disruption to my study time.

I was obsessed by a sense of being behind. I barely watched TV or listened to music. I was staying up past midnight and waking early to study.

One morning, my Home Class teacher, Mr Robinson, pulled me aside as the other students went to their first period.

'Are you okay, Corey?'

'Yeah.'

'You look very tired. Everything all right?'

What could I say to him? How could he help? Even if I broke down and told him how if I didn't get good marks I'd be nothing, be cast back into that horrible anonymous poverty I had grown up in, what could he do? Say, 'You can come and live with me at my house'?

'Just didn't get much sleep last night.'

'Okay. Just know that I'm here.'

After school I went to the library and studied until they kicked us out. I'd go back to my room, studying until my desk light was the sole one on in the dorm and someone would inevitably yell out for me to switch it off. Then I'd grab a blanket from my bed and throw it over the top of my cubicle, check no light was leaking out, and carefully wriggle into my cocoon to continue working.

'Corey,' a voice said. I looked up from my homework to see Richard Lim in my doorway.

'Hi, man,' I said.

'Can you help me with my English assignment, please?'

'I'm sorry but I really need to work on my assignment.'

'No help?'

'I'm sorry.'

The guy had rich parents in Hong Kong; who cared if he failed English? He'd be fine. Foster care had taught me the truth of the world: look after only yourself. Ultimately, nobody would be there for you, so why bother being there for anyone else? I felt myself boil with rage. I hated Richard, hated that his parents were rich enough to send him to school in a country where he barely spoke the language, hated that he dared to ask me for help when he'd been given all the help in the world.

'Two minutes,' he pleaded, holding up two fingers.

'Mate, I can't help you, I've got my own work to do.'

He looked at me with a sour expression and angrily darted through the curtain out of my room. I felt no regret. It was every boy for himself.

I was at Nudgee on an equity bursary because of the best part of the Catholic tradition: its emphasis on social justice. Yet I didn't have time to help a kid who needed help. It was selfishness borne of abandonment. I had been conditioned to take as much as I could and give as little back as possible. Nobody, I told myself, gave a shit about me. Why should I care about anyone else?

Nothing about me was good enough. My genes, my heritage, my life. Even when I won academic medals, I felt embarrassed for not being good enough. If only they knew how rotten and putrid and false I was, they would spit on me, place my mouth on a gutter and stomp on my disgusting head.

I thought I knew the reason people were disgusted by me. It was my teeth. Really my jawline. Actually it was my whole head. Frequently I'd look at myself in the mirror and think, *That's a criminal-shaped head. Of course people aren't comfortable around you.*

I didn't know it, but I had internalised Tracey, had inhaled her poisonous commands until they became the very voice inside my head. I had duplicated her inside myself.

Josh and Steven had become more vicious.

Sometimes they threw cream buns at me during lunch. I tried to steer clear of them, came to dread lining up for food.

I wished I was more violent. I kept hoping my father's rage would be rekindled in me and I could turn it on them. Another cream bun landed a few centimetres from my shoes.

Once, I returned to the dorms after school to find my pillow was missing. I checked the floor in case I'd knocked it off my bed that morning but it was nowhere to be seen. Eventually I found it inside a toilet cubicle, atop the cistern.

Another time my thongs were stolen from my room, which meant showering barefoot on tiles you knew boys were jizzing and pissing on.

I was tiring of the practical jokes. I felt sorrier and sorrier for myself.

I couldn't think straight with the noise raging through the dorms. I'd bought several sets of earplugs but they were useless against the commotion, the music, yelling and laughing. And I didn't have good hearing – I couldn't understand how anybody else studied with all the racket.

BOUNCE. BOUNCE. BOUNCE.

What sort of animal bounced a basketball indoors?

I stuck my head into the doorway. It was Nelson, casually strolling around.

'Hey Nelson, would it be okay if you bounced that somewhere else?'

'Oh,' he said, far too empathetically. 'Sorry.'

'Thanks,' I said, knowing what was coming next. I'd barely pulled my head back through the curtain when the bouncing started again. From the sound of it, he had moved even closer to my room.

I stuck my head back out. 'Hey, Nelson, sorry to be a hassle but could you bounce the ball somewhere else, please?'

'Oh,' he chuckled, 'sorry.'

Before I had even sat down again, I heard the BOUNCE. I thought about what I should do. There was no politeness, no respect. Should I resort to violence? To my mind he was trying to ruin my life. To destroy my chances of making something of myself. I was trying my fucking hardest to do well and here was Nelson, some VET student, who didn't even need Nudgee to do what he wanted. Whatever happened, he'd go to TAFE and pick up an apprenticeship in the mines. And if that failed, he had his family, who evidently were wealthy enough to send him to a boarding school.

BOUNCE.

Desperate times called for desperate measures.

I spoke with Des, our hall monitor. The kind of softly spoken giant you got the sense might contain an anger so profound that, if it ever appeared, could very well end in a man's mashed face dripping through his hands.

'Hey, Des, I'm really struggling to study in here.'

'Yeah, the boys won't listen to anyone. I'm struggling with it too, mate.'

'Do you reckon I could use that room at the end of that corridor to study in?'

'What room's that?'

'I'll show you,' I said and led him down another wing, around a corner and to a door which I'd never seen open.

'I can study here,' I announced.

'Hmm,' Des pondered, trying a key in the lock. He fumbled for a little while until finally the door swung inwards to reveal a neat room with a solitary desk and chair.

'This is wonderful,' I said in awe. It was perfectly noiseless. I couldn't hear anything the other boarders were doing. It was the ideal study nook.

'Make sure you lock the room when you're done,' Des said.

For a few weeks, I studied in peace.

I never found out how he'd discovered my monastery, but Nick Wadeson was the first to do so. One night I heard a knock at the door. I opened it a fraction and saw Nick standing there, textbooks, pads and pencil case tucked under his arm.

'Hey, Whitey, mind if I study here too?'

'I sure do,' is what I wanted to say. Instead I waved him inside with a smile. 'Nah, you're welcome.' When he was inside, I locked the door. 'Nick, I don't mind you coming in here, but you can't tell anyone about this. This is the last bastion of study.'

Over time a few other guys joined us. The little air-conditioned room became a refugee camp for those of us who cared about our grades. Soon there were five or six guys stretched out in the room desperate to learn. Word quickly spread and I regretted my generosity.

It all came to an end too quickly when I asked Des to let me into the room one afternoon and Lionel Wilson, a fat Shar-Pei of a boy, was sprawled sleeping on a mattress in the room, his white belly quivering with his snores.

'Lionel,' said Des.

'What's happening?' Lionel asked bleary-eyed.

'You're not supposed to be in here,' Des said sternly.

'It was too hot to sleep in the dorms last night.'

Eventually Mr Hughes stepped in. At a dorm meeting he announced that the room was not to be used any more.

'Mr Hughes,' I explained in his office, 'I really need that room to study. The dorms are too noisy.'

'Well, they shouldn't be. Let me have a chat with the hall monitors and we'll get the noise down.'

I looked at his bovine, friendly face with its froggy dewlap and silver moustache and didn't feel reassured.

My instinct was correct. The dorms only grew more cacophonous. The inmates were well and truly running the asylum.

Boys now openly flouted the required silence of study time. Groups of them would spend the allotted two hours passing a football around immediately outside my room. Peeking through a gap in the curtain, I saw Des passing a football around. Noble, dignified Des whom I had thought an ally against the VET students, who had seemed to sympathise with my hunger to do well, had now been charmed by the animals.

I tried more expensive earplugs but they didn't work. Stereos blared, people playing James Blunt's 'You're Beautiful' and shouting cut through the foam like I wanted to cut through every lousy fucker with a sword. I stayed up later and later to study, poring over textbooks until the words seemed like hieroglyphics. I'd go to bed at 3 and be woken up at 7.30.

'You should relax,' Donald said one night.

'I've gotta study,' I said without looking up from my textbook.

The thought of relaxing struck me as the most disgusting, lazy thing I could imagine.

The Simpsons was *the* cultural touchstone for my generation, but I'd barely watched it. A succession of foster families wouldn't let me. I missed out on the richest vein of references available to my peers, and all through school I resented others for being able to quote it.

At Nudgee, quotes from *The Simpsons* functioned as prosthetic personalities.

'Don't you know the "Talkin' Softball" lyrics?' said Nigel, sneering at me. 'Everybody knows.' I looked at his white face. He was the Platonic ideal of a rich kid. Porcelain skin, icy blue eyes, straight brown hair. I could sense his desire to crush me, to humiliate me.

'You're not even funny, dude,' I said. 'You just remember a funny thing on *The Simpsons*. You're a comedy parasite.'

'Boom,' whooped Tom Martin, lifting his hands as if a grenade had exploded. His mother worked in the laundry yet nobody ever brought this fact up. 'Burned by C-unit.' Nigel's face reddened.

'You're an idiot, Corey. Why don't you wash your pants, you grub?'

I thought about saying something like, 'Because Tom's mum already has enough laundry to do,' but decided against it. It'd hurt Nigel by association, but Tom had done nothing terrible himself. He'd just witnessed Nigel's dick-swinging, like a secretary to a Nazi officer.

Plus Nigel was right about my pants. They were filthy. For months

I'd been so focused on schoolwork I'd stopped going to drop off clothes at the laundry. I didn't have time to waste. I looked down at my shorts. I could smell my balls through them, and I noticed dandruff on them. I reminded myself I should shampoo my hair, until I realised I'd run out of shampoo. I'd have to walk to the shops, a few minutes down the road. I had two assignments due in the next week so I wouldn't have time. It'd have to wait. Besides, it wasn't that much dandruff, you could barely notice.

School holidays in my room at Clyde House were lonely. While I had separated from the general social life at boarding school, there was something comforting about the buzz of the dorms, the sense of belonging. The edge of vital activity made you feel less lonely.

I'd lie in my room thinking of how the other boarders at Nudgee were spending their holiday. Probably yachting, on vacation in Europe or fucking a prostitute their parents hired for them to practise sex with.

I spent as little time with the residents and workers of Clyde House as I could. I considered them losers, inconvenient reminders of what I had come from, and was afraid of being infected by their lack of ambition and contentment with their lot. I locked myself in my room, reading my textbooks from the previous term, consolidating my knowledge and redoing quizzes, emerging only for meals.

———

I discovered Friedrich Nietzsche on the shelves of the school library. I fell in love with him, devouring as many of his books as I could. Much of it was too advanced for me, but I drew close to it instinctively. His concept of the will to power struck me as true. The idea that people simply wanted to be powerful and shape the world in the way they wanted provided an explanation. Unconsciously, it provided an answer for my abuse in foster care, why what had happened had happened. More than that, it also offered a way to live my life. I decided that I wanted to be powerful.

Matt wanted power. Tracey wanted power. My father wanted power. Everybody wanted power, and what had I been doing acting any other way? It made everything less personal.

Hadn't I always known that people were shit? Untrustworthy, bloodthirsty, lazy, pathetic? I could see the thread of hoping people would be kind to me running through my life, how it had let me down. I had stayed with Tracey for years, despite everything, because I had hoped she would change.

I had been so weak. My hunger for mercy so pitiable. The truth was you couldn't rely on anyone. No golden time would ever come. Life would always be hard and cruel. This was The Truth.

It wasn't negative or pessimistic. It was liberating. People weren't good or evil. They were simply doing what made them feel powerful. This was a great comfort. People were like earthquakes and leukaemia; none of it was personal.

I didn't care any more about the noise in the dorms. I even kept the curtain to my room open. They would not be polite if I asked them; I could not fight them. All that was left to do was take on the burden and just keep going. The struggle made me better.

I felt I was finally seeing things clearly. I would not be a wounded animal any longer. I was strong. I was holding up against unremitting brutality. I would never break; I would prevail despite everything. At last I was facing reality.

Nietzsche was my Oprah. All difficulty and conflict was fertile soil for greatness. My survival was proof I was destined for something greater than all this.

My sense of alienation from others became a source of pride: pain inverted into glory. I was better than them; obviously I wouldn't get along with them. Through a sleight of hand, Nietzsche's maxim that what doesn't kill you makes you stronger meant I welcomed isolation.

Now when I attended Mass I sneered at Christ on the Cross. It must have made a strange sight: a foster child on an equity scholarship at a Catholic boarding school decrying Christianity as a slave morality. The mad blind irony of it makes me laugh now.

I marched grimly through the year, earning top marks, accumulating academic medals. I could feel the heaviness of my eyeballs in their sockets. I went days without showering. But I knew I was strong enough. I could take it. I had survived, I would continue to survive. I would prosper.

It was now time to submit our university course preferences. I'd decided I wanted to study Computer Science after a term spent reading a few books on artificial intelligence, figuring that was where I could make my mark. I wanted to help give birth to something better than humanity.

———

As I packed up my room to leave Nudgee, the last of my energy from that year of exhaustive work draining out of me, I felt hollow.

A social worker from Clyde House came to pick me up. Driving away from Nudgee for the last time, I looked out the window and thought back to when I'd first arrived. I remembered the tremendous promise of it all.

I knew I'd likely never see any of the boys again. I'd made the choices I had to, but a part of me wished I hadn't. I imagined walking into a school reunion in twenty years and awkwardly milling about on the edge of the group, picking at pastries, making it seem I was a glutton rather than a no-friends Nigel who'd mistakenly attended a reunion. I envisioned myself waving at random spaces in the room and pointing to the pastries and back at the random space so that anyone looking at me would think I was temporarily inconvenienced by a mini-quiche instead of devoted to it.

'Well done, Corey.'

'Thanks.'

I hoped my OP score was good enough to get into university. If it wasn't, I didn't know what I'd do. I was turning eighteen in a little under two months, when I'd be released from foster care. The Nudgee Equity Office had arranged a scholarship to board at a university college, though this was contingent on me attending university to begin with.

The notion of not going to university was unthinkable.

I spent the summer in a frenzy of self-improvement, running through the streets surrounding Clyde House for kilometres until lactic acid forced me to my knees; reading books until my eyes stung.

I yearned to be perfect, physically and mentally. I'd bought a stack of computer programming books but dared not start learning how to code until I knew I was going to university. It was all I could do to distract myself from the horrific possibility of failure.

Then one morning Eileen called out from the lounge room, 'Mail for you, Corey. From Nudgee!'

I tore open the large white envelope, pulled out the wad of documents inside and rifled through them for the only one that mattered. Suddenly there it was, in my hand, plain yet special. I scanned for the magic number.

OP3.

The third-highest possible score, twenty-two places above the lowest score, OP25. I'd even been awarded Dux of Geography from Nudgee. It was easily enough to ensure I'd be accepted to study my first preference at university, Information Technology majoring in Computer Science.

'Three! Three! I'm going to university!' I lifted Eileen clean off the floor and swung her around then put her down when my back started hurting.

She punched the air and squeezed me. 'I'm so happy for you.'

Two years of sacrificing everything on the altar of study had paid off. I had no friends and was deeply lonely, but it didn't matter. Nothing else mattered because I had the grades I needed.

'I have to start learning computer programming right away,' I said, heading back to my room.

Now I would conquer university.

8

I turned eighteen without any fanfare. There was no birthday cake or raucous party. It was not a momentous day for me. It just meant I was a little closer to continuing my ascent through the world.

There was no paperwork or pomp from the Department either. I received no special letter from the Queen or the Government celebrating my survival. The State was now as free of me as I was of it. This provoked almost no emotion in me, though. Bureaucracies were inarguable. You might as well get upset by the width of a parking space.

Normally Clyde House residents were required to leave on the day of their eighteenth birthday but Eileen had received special dispensation for me to stay on for a couple of weeks until I moved into St Leo's College, the residence I'd be living in on campus.

Until learning I'd received marks good enough to attend university, I'd feared turning eighteen. It was well known among children in care that the Department simply severed its relationship with you when you became an adult.

I'd had no idea what I would do without university to go to.

I was obsessed with preparations for my new life. I'd busily been studying the curriculum over the holidays, borrowing books from the library and working through maths quizzes and computer programming challenges.

Loneliness broke through occasionally. I hadn't kept friends from Nudgee – but I knew that university would be different. There would be a higher calibre of person there. University, I was sure, would be filled with my people, golden intellectuals and such.

There would be women too, whom I also began improving myself for. I spent months pumping weights and going for long runs in anticipation of the toga parties to come. I had even begun to memorise poetry – Shakespeare's sonnets, e.e. cummings, and T. S. Eliot's *The Waste Land* – which I stored up, rehearsing them in the mirror for a day not too far away when I would kneel beside a beautiful woman on a picnic blanket and rattle them off to swooning and kisses.

I had some vague plan of becoming a handsome professor of computer science. I'd wear pastel turtlenecks and gleaming brown leather shoes, smoke cigars on Chesterfield wing chairs, and decry the parlous state of digital infrastructure. I held this image of myself in my head like mental fentanyl.

Eileen helped me move into St Leo's. Over the course of several trips, we shifted my things from the van to my room, all while she warbled about how nice the room was and how she was so proud of me. We exchanged our hopes about our futures. I wanted to continue my success at university and beyond, while she and Buzz were looking to retire from residential youth work.

When we had finished, Eileen stood, pigeon-toed, beaming at me. 'You're going to change the world, mister.'

We hugged and said goodbye.

When the door shut behind Eileen, I felt a tremendous sense of emptiness. I would miss her. I already missed her. Before she'd left the room, she had told me I was welcome to call her any time, handing me a strip of paper with her personal mobile number on it. I had to fight the urge to call her immediately and ask her to take me back to Clyde House.

At five o'clock, new residents were summoned to the main hall of the college for an official welcome ceremony. There were nearly a hundred of us in total, plus a few dozen parents who'd stayed to support their sons. The Rector of St Leo's gave a long speech about life on campus, following which he invited parents to say goodbye to their children. Sons shook their father's hands and suffered the kisses of their mothers. Then the parents filed out, along with the school administration.

The St Leo's Student Club, composed of third-year students, took to the stage. Their presentations were less polished than the administration's. The sports co-ordinator spoke, along with the culture and social co-ordinators. After a brief, virtually inaudible speech by a nervous vice-president, finally the president of the student club stood before us.

'What we like to do at St Leo's College is to make first years feel welcome,' droned the president, a tall blond man with slightly bulging eyes. 'So what we're going to do is ask you to hold hands while we sing our college song.'

Incredulity swept through us. What the hell? Holding hands and singing? He may as well have asked us to engage in anal play with our grandfathers. Begrudgingly, mutinously, we held hands.

An older boy walked onstage with an acoustic guitar and delivered it carefully into the arms of the president. He strummed a few times, looked up at us, then closed his eyes. 'Join with me as I sing, brothers. You'll figure out the words.'

As one, we exchanged furtive glances. Had we joined a cult?

The president's eyes flashed open briefly. 'Don't be shy, you're safe here. Sing, brothers, sing.'

We sang like Bosnian refugees singing the Serbian national anthem.

The vice-president stepped forward and, in an urgent, beatific voice, told us, 'Stand, brothers. We will sanctify the college with our singing!'

We rose awkwardly, still holding sweating hands with the boys beside us. We moved slowly forward as the president led us down a set of stairs to a basement beneath the hall.

One of the boys I was holding hands with whispered, 'This is fucked.'

When we had all been seated on the tiled floor of the basement, a bloodcurdling scream suddenly sliced through the air. To the left of us, a black curtain fell from the ceiling to reveal a bar. Simultaneously, the president reversed his hold on the guitar and swung it by the neck down to the ground, smashing it to smithereens. Meanwhile, a man dressed as the Phantom appeared behind the newly visible bar, clambered atop it, cupped his hands to his mouth, and bellowed, 'All right, you fresher maggots! Time to get fucked up!'

Around me boys threw each other's hands away and cheered wildly.

The next few hours were a cyclone of filth and depravity that still remains one of the best nights of drinking in my life. Nudgee's brotherly rituals had never completely gelled with me but this new incarnation of male bonding was one I could get behind.

I looked to my right and saw a pallid, rake-thin boy wearing glasses shot-gunning a can of XXXX while a senior leaned over him barking, 'Get that piss in your gullet, maggot!' Before long I too was shot-gunning a beer as a hulking, muscle-bound senior named Hercules instructed me, a fraction more gently, to do the same. The beer fizzed into my mouth and a semi-circle of boys screamed out for my success, which I celebrated by slamming the can down on the ground.

I vomited into a toilet twice. Boys were openly pissing on the floor and sculling beer from their shoes. Pizza was brought in, half of which was eaten, the other half becoming impromptu balls in a game of cricket which sprang up in the middle of the room.

I woke up the next morning to a massive thump on my door. 'Fresher! Touch footy! Now!' I staggered out of bed, cracked the door and stuck my head into the hallway. A few other boys were doing the same and we all turned to watch a senior banging on doors along the corridor.

'What's happening?' I croaked to the boy opposite me, who I was sure I'd seen tackle a bin the night before.

'Touch footy,' he said. 'I think we have to go play?'

'But I'm hungover. I'm gonna vomit.'

'I think that's the point,' he grinned.

For the first few months at St Leo's I felt part of a community, one of the boys. It was a new experience for me. Because we had our own locked rooms with thick wooden doors, and much more free time, I could study at my own pace, apportioning time to study and get on top of assessment pieces, which left my evenings more or less free for extra-curricular activities. The chessboard I'd brought to college remained unused on my desk, attracting first a film of dust then a stack of papers and books.

I attended my tutorials and lectures diligently, completed homework religiously. I was surprised to find the work easy and was grateful I'd spent the summer studying the material ahead of time. I received the highest marks possible for all of my courses. It was a breeze.

And alcohol was a nice social lubricant that quickly dissolved my awkwardness. Getting drunk levelled social hierarchies. As long as you were prepared to swig beer at the drop of a hat, you were welcome to drink among others, if only for that night in the pub. If you could make yourself a beast, you were equal with the rest.

At the end of my first semester, other boys returned to their homes for the holiday break, while I stayed on since the college was now my permanent home.

I spent the first few days sleeping, and then began looking over the courses I'd be taking for second semester. They filled me with dread. The mathematics course I'd be studying was byzantine gobbledegook I wasn't sure I could master. Maybe I'd been wrong to choose to do the Information Technology degree? I buried the doubt and spent the remaining week and a half of my break preparing for the semester.

When classes resumed, my apprehension lingered. I was studying as hard as I could, but my motivation was dipping. I started missing a few classes here and there in favour of sleeping, figuring I could catch up later. Pretty soon I skipped a whole week, then two.

It became clear that the first semester had been easier than I'd expected because I had spent months preparing for it, and because the subjects had been the easiest ones in my degree.

Simultaneously, I felt a growing disconnect between me and the other boys at St Leo's. Friends and drinking buddies still knocked on my door to invite me to go out, but I declined them repeatedly. Eventually, the offers dried up.

A point came when I decided that any further socialising with them was a wasted investment. The golden future I'd dreamed of would have to be delayed until after I'd finished university. I just had too much going on. The old resentment of those who had it easier than me found its way back into my thinking.

I tried to kill the part of me that wanted friendship and connection. It weakened me at precisely the time when I needed to study like a machine. If I didn't get good enough marks at university to secure a career, where would I end up? Probably one of the hunched, wizened cleaners who swept through the college to clean each morning, mopping vomit, piss and shit from bathrooms and the college bar, suffering the patronising friendliness of young men in the midst of forging prosperous lives.

A month into this new semester, I was finding it increasingly difficult to concentrate. My mind, a laser at Nudgee, focusing through months of decreased sleep and five-hour study sessions, had now decayed into a dim, blinking light. Simple tasks like reading a chapter in a textbook seemed insurmountable. It was also becoming harder to summon the energy to leave my room and go to university lectures and tutorials.

A new and horrible fear pierced me: had I inherited my father's bipolar disorder? Was this fading of my powers of focus the beginning of a disabling mental illness? Was this how he had begun on his path to being that doughy idiot I'd met in Department headquarters all those years ago?

I booked an appointment with the campus psychiatrist and explained my symptoms and family history.

'Is there a chance I have bipolar disorder?' I asked.

He told me that it sounded like I was experiencing the early stages of depression, but bipolar disorder also included periods of mania.

'What are the symptoms of mania?' I asked.

He rattled off a list: inflated self-esteem, grandiosity, reduced need for sleep, heightened confidence, irritability, poor impulse control, racing thoughts.

I told him I thought I might have experienced manic periods. I vaguely remembered my father took lithium. 'If I have bipolar disorder, I'll have to take lithium, right?'

'Yes.'

'Well, I'm happy to do whatever I must in order to stay functional.'

He scrawled out a prescription and handed it to me. 'The way it's going to work is it will level you out. It will mean you won't go off the deep end during a manic episode or have disabling depression.'

'Good,' I said. Conscious of how much work remained to be done, I made to leave.

'But,' the psychiatrist continued, the word freezing me like thunder. 'Lithium does have some side effects you need to know about. Weight gain. Sleepiness. You might have difficulty concentrating.'

The last point was a hammer blow. 'Difficulty concentrating?'

'Yes. Some people find that taking lithium means they can't think or focus as well.'

I leaned back in the chair, deflated. 'But I need to concentrate for university. That's the whole problem.'

The psychiatrist paused. 'I understand, Corey. However, if you have bipolar disorder, you need to accept the idea that it will affect your life in ways you don't like.'

This was unacceptable. I hadn't come this far – through foster care and Nudgee and the beginning of university – only to be slowed down and forced to give up on my dreams. My mind flitted over everything, searching for a way out.

'Maybe I don't have bipolar disorder?' I said. 'Maybe I've exaggerated my symptoms of mania.'

Across from me the psychiatrist considered the turn in conversation. 'That is definitely a possibility. However, you need to take the medication and see if there's a relief in symptoms and then we can reassess.'

The lithium didn't help. I became sleepier and my concentration worsened, while motivation seemed to leak out of me on an hourly basis. After a month I quit, stuffing the bottle in the drawer of my desk, consequences be damned.

A fog was closing in but I did everything I could to blast it away. Terrified of losing my hunger to succeed, I found new levers inside myself to operate. I didn't want to be a worthless piece of shit, did I? I wasn't lazy, was I?

The negative self-talk drove me out of bed and into lecture theatres and tutorials. In my room, bent over my desk, I tripled the amount of time I spent reading textbooks and answering problems. Any time my focus wavered, I brought it back to the ink on the page and the pixels on the computer screen.

Don't be lazy, you dumb fuck.

Don't be a disgusting slob.

Don't be a pathetic idiot.

These recriminations were a new tool that kept my sickness at bay. They worked and by semester's end I'd maintained my perfect grades.

The rest of the college packed down their rooms and headed home for the two months until university recommenced.

I collapsed from exhaustion. The fog rolled in and in, all the way in until the only thing I could see was that I was fading away.

Since Nudgee, excelling in academia had been my north star. The end of the university year and the weeks of holidays ahead left me with nothing to strive for. Now my world was starless.

I holed up in my room. I stopped showering. I grew sicker.

I stayed in bed from the time I woke to the time I slept again, discrete states that soon blended to form a hybrid dissociative waking nightmare.

It seemed so unfair, a cosmic injustice. I had worked so hard and sacrificed so much trying to make something of myself, but now my father's illness had come for me.

It was pointless to continue studying my Information Technology degree, or any degree at all. I had wanted to achieve something great with my life, but why bother now?

Weeks of rumination in my lightless, stinking room capsized me. I plunged into an existential crisis. What was the meaning of life? What was the meaning of life? What was the meaning of life?

If it wasn't striving for excellence, what was it? Friendship and happiness? I knew they weren't available to me. Maybe at one point I'd had friends, but not now, not after I'd closed myself off from others. And the possibility of my own happiness seemed laughable. I knew my childhood had fucked me up, that I was different to others. Deep down, I wasn't a real person. Something was missing in me. Others found me strange. I disgusted them in a way they were too kind to admit.

I waited for something to save me, the way admission to Nudgee once had. I prayed to a God I didn't believe in to rescue me. I was met by silence.

———

Time passed by in an eventless sludge. Christmas and New Year's Eve came and went.

The only occasions when I left my room were to piss, shit or go to the college kitchen of an evening to pick up one plate piled up massively with food I'd pick at until the following evening. I kept the filthy plates beside my bed in growing stacks, which in turn attracted ants that crawled over me as I slept, biting me and leaving their acrid stench on my skin. When they woke me, at first I killed them, but after a while I couldn't be bothered and let them crawl over my flesh to their destination.

I spent my nineteenth birthday alone in my room without talking to a single person.

I don't remember deciding to kill myself. It was instinct. I sank towards suicide the way flowers seek the sun.

I sat down at my desk and fetched the bottle of lithium pills from my drawer and poured all thirty or forty of them into my palm. I shovelled them into my mouth, gagging at the metallic taste. I gulped a glass of orange juice and forced myself to swallow them. My hands were covered in a thin film of lithium dust which I licked clean to ensure a toxic dose.

I reclined on my sheetless mattress and waited to fade away. This was it. This was how I was going to leave the world. Nineteen years old, alone in a filthy room, ants crawling up the walls, listening to Enya.

Suddenly, I had an overwhelming desire to vomit. I fought it for a few seconds but it was too strong. I ran down the hallway to the bathroom, shoved my head into a toilet bowl and spewed up the pills. I lurched back to bed and fell asleep, unsure of whether I'd wake up.

I came to the next morning, neither grateful nor disappointed. My mind was blank, nothing but stillness. Beyond wanting life or death. Devoid of any thoughts or feelings, it had come to a merciful halt.

9

The rest of the college returned from holidays tanned, excited, wild, hungry for bacchanal. I remained in my room and when the term commenced I didn't attend any lectures or classes, or submit assignments or sit exams.

Occasionally I would go out drinking with boys from college, and invariably, these nights followed an identical, sloppy pattern. We would arrive at a pub, where I'd feel a rising sense of unease at tagging along, being out of place. To quell it, I'd drink heavily – very heavily – downing three drinks to each of theirs. Within an hour, I'd have had eight drinks as they nursed their third. In this sodden state, my spiritual troubles came burping out.

'Hey, Nugget,' I'd slur at a boy, who might not even be called Nugget. I'd forgotten many people's names and would often be corrected with a stinging rebuke.

'Hey, Corey,' he'd say warily.

'What do you think is the meaning of life?' I'd ask earnestly.

Usually, my interlocutor would answer that they didn't know or, more commonly, that they didn't care. I'd hiccup on about my 'long dark night of the soul' and at some point they'd tell me they had to go give a parking inspector a massage.

Within ninety minutes of a drinking session beginning, I'd be on my way home, after vomiting, usually on myself, sometimes in a pot plant if I was lucky. Boys would gently put me into a taxi back to college, a ceremony of fussing I secretly enjoyed.

One night, as the final stretch of semester approached, I was out at the university student pub and struck up a conversation with a girl at the bar.

'What do you think is the meaning of life?' I asked her, as the bartender slid my beer to me and collected the five-dollar note I'd slapped down.

'I don't know,' the girl said, sipping a vodka sunrise through a straw. 'It's something I struggle with. What do you think?'

I was momentarily taken aback by the reciprocal angst. Nobody had ever engaged with me before. 'I don't know, I'm looking for it. But right now, I don't know what the point is. Why go on? Why do anything at all?'

The girl smiled. She was wearing a black dress, the same colour as her shoulder-length hair, in striking contrast to her alabaster skin.

We kept talking. She invited me outside for a cigarette and, though I didn't smoke, I agreed. It was the first time in a long time I'd felt any sort of connection to another person.

She departed soon after, promising to contact me by email. I returned to my room at college infatuated by her.

The next morning, good to her word, Nina emailed me and we began a long correspondence. We talked for weeks about our mutual depression. She was obsessed with Jeff Buckley and sent me links to his music, proclaiming him a genius, the most tragic and handsome figure in musical history. She was madly in love with him, she said. I was madly in love with her and listened dutifully to every song of his she sent through to me.

We messaged each other every day, sharing tidbits from our lives, updating one another on precisely where we were in our descent into the abyss. It was terribly romantic and important.

When Nina was offline, I fantasised about being with her. We could be two doomed lovers in a world blotted by death and loneliness. I tried to summon the courage to ask her out for a drink but never could. I resorted instead to hoping she would extend me an invitation, if only based on the sheer number of Jeff Buckley songs she'd told me I must listen to.

At last, it came. Did I, she wrote, want to go clubbing with her and, maybe, take ecstasy together?

I agreed in a heartbeat and the date was set.

Friday night rolled around and my phone rang.

'Just outside, in the car park.' It was Nina's voice, soft and feminine, which I hadn't heard since the night we met.

'Coming now!' I sang. I skipped out of my room and down the stairs, slowing to a dispassionate stroll as I approached the bitumen lot.

'Hey, Corey, over here,' shouted Nina from the passenger's side of a navy sedan.

'Hey,' I said, jumping into the back seat.

'Hello,' Nina chirped, turning around and smiling at me.

A young blond guy sat in the driver's seat. 'I'm Tim,' he said through the rear-view mirror.

I was a little thrown. I had thought it was just going to be me and Nina.

'You ready for the best night of your life?' Nina asked.

Tim parked around the corner from the club and Nina began to distribute the ecstasy from a small zip-lock bag.

She dropped a small green pill into my hand, her finger brushing my palm. I watched her throw hers beyond her glossy, bee-stung pink lips. She fetched a bottle of Mount Franklin water from the cupholder and I watched her thin wrist twist elegantly as she took a sip.

She looked across at Tim in the driver's seat. 'Did you do yours?'

'Yes,' he said.

'You sure?' she asked. He stuck his tongue out as proof. 'Good,' flirted Nina. Then, in a far less flirty tone, she asked, 'What about you, Corey?'

'No. Can I have your water?' I felt as wanted as a cleaner knocking on the door of a hotel room.

'Sure,' piped Nina and handed it to me.

I washed the pill down and took a sip, tasting Nina's lip gloss on the mouth of the bottle.

'Okay! Let's do this,' she said.

We locked the car and strolled in the direction of Nina's behest. She and Tim were chatting casually, like old friends. They seemed to have a pre-existing relationship of some depth. I tagged along behind them, feeling foolish.

'Are you feeling anything yet?' Tim asked me across Nina.

'Not yet,' I said.

'Same here,' he smiled.

'I don't either,' Nina chipped in.

'Well,' said Tim, 'it takes about half an hour to kick in. Let's stick together and make sure we all have a good time.'

At least he wasn't an arsehole.

There was absolutely no chance Nina wasn't madly in love with Tim. She would not be my dark nihilistic queen. As I walked, listening to them discuss the cover charge at the club we were going to, I had a further dagger-like realisation that Tim bore an uncanny resemblance to Jeff Buckley. I ran my hand along my stubby jaw and rued my genetic misfortune.

The nightclub rose up before us. 'Oh my God,' Nina squealed, resting her head on my shoulder. 'We're here! I'm so excited!' I nearly passed out from the scent of her perfume. Mercifully, she danced ahead to pay her entry fee. Tim followed her and I followed him, comparing the width of his shoulders with photos I'd seen of Jeff Buckley.

A haggard woman stamped my wrist once I'd handed over the twenty dollars for entry and said, 'Welcome. Party safely.'

I dropped to my knees in the middle of the dance floor, unable to speak except to gasp, 'Oh my God, oh my God.' How was it possible to even feel this great? Six months of depression had been blasted away, and everything was beautiful and true and good.

For the first time in six months I felt alive.

Tim lifted me in a bear hug, put me down, then grabbed my face. 'It's marvellous, isn't it?'

'It's a fucking miracle!'

I let my head roll back heavenward as the bliss washed through me, my feet stomping to the beat.

I skipped back to Tim and Nina and said, 'Can we do this every weekend, please?'

'Of course,' they said, pulling me into a group hug.

Nina and Tim began passionately kissing against a railing. I stared at them, admiring how beautiful they were. They pulled away and opened their eyes. Nina noticed me looking at them and yelled, 'Corey!' She reached out with her gorgeous arm and took my hand and pulled me towards them.

'This is heaven,' I sputtered in joy, dancing with her.

'It is,' she cried. The fairytale escalated when Nina moved forward and kissed me on the lips, her tongue finding mine. I closed my eyes and pressed my body to her. When we stopped kissing I saw Tim hovering beside her, looking at me longingly. Handsome Jeff Buckley Tim. I leaned forward and pressed my lips to his, willing him to feel wanted and blessed.

Tim kissed me and Nina kissed me. Tim sucked on my ear, which sent new feelings of pleasure through my body. I returned the favour. Our bodies blended in the throbbing cavernous room filled with green lasers spinning over every surface.

I danced away. 'This is heaven!' I yelled again as I threw my hands in the air in a paltry gesture of gratitude to the universe.

I felt a strong urge to take my shirt off so I did. Why shouldn't I,

I was handsome! I leapt on to the dance platform and gyrated to the electro. People looked up at me and I felt electric with revelation. Overlooking it, I saw the dance floor in a new way. We were all dancing, and the totality of our dancing was itself a dance. I felt it didn't matter if I died, because the dance would go on. In an immortal gestalt, the world gleamed holy.

I intuited that I had to continue dancing to keep the darkness at bay. For hours, I stomped and shuffled around the dance floor, sweating profusely, swigging water from a bottle.

Why wasn't everybody doing ecstasy all the time? For breakfast, lunch and dinner?

After a few hours, the ecstasy started to wear off, replaced by bubbling anxiety.

Tim and I sat on a couch watching Nina dance. She stood in one spot, twisting slowly, her arms above her, eyes closed in inward nirvana.

I thought about the fact that we had had our tongues down each other's throats and I felt uneasy, which I chalked up to the dreaded 'comedown' that everyone described on the internet.

Nina came and sat between me and Tim. I watched her curl into him and begin sobbing into his chest.

'Are you okay?' I asked.

Tim's head emerged from her hair. 'We just need to have a chat.'

'Okay,' I said, taking the hint.

I wandered back out onto the dance floor again, grimy from my dry sweat. I tried to summon the ecstatic feelings of an hour before but couldn't.

I crawled onto my bed, bent my pillow over itself, and the moment my head hit it, I was out. I slept through the next day and when I woke in the evening darkness, I was revitalised. Last night had been perfect. Life didn't mean anything, a horrifying vacuum sat hollow inside everything, but drugs made me feel good. It was indisputable, like *cogito ergo sum* and 1+1=2. In one night, I'd been transformed from lost melancholic to drug fiend.

I messaged Nina thanking her for the night and asked if she wanted to go out again the coming Friday. She didn't reply until a few days later, when she wrote to say that she was rotten sick. Her comedown was so bad she'd not been able to leave her room. I said I was sorry that she was having a hard time and wished her a quick recovery.

A few minutes later, I sent her a follow-up message. 'Is there any way I could buy some of the you know what from the other night?'

She didn't reply, and a few nights later I found myself in the same nightclub, alone this time. I walked through the writhing, gyrating revellers. My plan was to ask somebody if they knew how I could get drugs.

'Hi there,' I said to one woman dancing with her head bent down to her knees as she shook her behind in the air like a jubilant bee. 'Hi there,' I shouted once more over the music.

She didn't hear me, lost in exultation.

I moved away from her to a man in a singlet and slim-fit black jeans with white sneakers. He was lathered in sweat, pumping his fists in the air to the pounding electronic music. 'Hey, mate,' I shouted.

'What's up, buddy?' he yelled over the music.

'Do you know where I can get ecstasy?'

'Sorry, buddy, I pre-dropped.' Before he'd even finished the sentence, I was moving towards another possible target, a morbidly obese man, a crown of sweat slipping down his face as he clapped and stomped on the wooden floor. I figured he must be either in the throes of chemical bliss or a Christian preacher trying to cast the devil out of the nightclub.

I stepped in front of him and waved for his attention. He stopped and grinned at me. 'Do you know anyone with ecstasy?' I shouted.

'I love you,' he shouted back, seizing me in a sweaty embrace which I ducked away from.

I spent a half hour pinballing around the dance floor, ricocheting from one rejection to another. Nobody had any leads, or at least they wouldn't tell me. In hindsight, I may well have looked like an undercover cop.

I was readying myself to approach a group of women energetically dancing in a circle around their handbags when somebody tapped me on the shoulder. I turned and saw a towering bouncer who shook his blocky head and motioned for me to come with him. I complied, trailing him through the club and out onto the street.

'What's wrong?' I asked.

'We've been watching you bother people and we don't want you here.'

'Excuse me but I'm a customer. I spent twenty dollars to come in.' I shook the stamp on my wrist at him indignantly.

'Mate,' the behemoth drawled, 'you were asking people for drugs. This is not a drugs nightclub.'

I scoffed. 'Have you seen people's pupils in there? They're clearly on drugs.'

'No they're not,' he said. 'Their pupils are big because it's dark so they've expanded to absorb more light.' He held his chin up in victory, staring down his meaty nose.

'Can I at least get a refund on my entry fee?'

'No.'

'What a horrible way to treat a loyal customer! I won't be coming here again,' I huffed and stormed off.

I wandered agitated through the streets searching for another nightclub, before I stumbled upon a place called The Beat, which appeared to be a gay bar if the queue of slim men in tight black shirts, white suspenders and bright pink shorts was anything to go by. I decided to try my luck here and stood behind two women in flannelette shirts holding hands. The line crawled forward. The bouncer glanced at me, nodded approvingly and waved me through to the booth.

'Hi there, how much is the cover charge?' I asked a bored-looking man in a tight white vest.

'It's free until 10 o'clock, hon. Go on up.'

I mounted a set of stairs, taking in the tacky décor. Wood-panelled walls, gaudy blue-red-yellow carpet, garish neon signs, a multitude of cheap-looking photographs of naked men. This, I thought, was encouraging. Someone in a dive like this had to sell ecstasy.

Burned by my unsuccessful attempts to procure drugs on the dance floor, I decided to change tack and hang out in the beer garden. When I'd done ecstasy with Nina and Tim, we'd headed out for cigarettes periodically and most of the other smokers had been chewing their faces off, casually talking about how they'd taken this pill and smoked this substance. The smoker's section therefore seemed to be an ideal location to find drug contacts instead of my Mr Bean-esque method of asking dozens of random people in full view of security staff.

I bought a beer from the bar and took it out to the smoking area, sitting by myself in the corner nervously.

'Hello, cutie,' a tubby middle-aged man in a leather vest said, plonking himself down beside me. 'Why are you sitting here by yourself?'

I mumbled something about fresh air.

'I'm Bryan.' He offered his hand.

I shook it. 'I'm Corey.'

'That's a cute name.'

'Thanks.'

I sensed his eyes slither over me. He slid closer, pressing his leg against mine. 'You out with friends?'

'No.'

'What are you here for then?' he asked sidling a little closer.

I noticed his belly stretching his black leather vest and glimpsed his floppy chest, with both nipples pierced. I made a line call that Bryan wasn't part of this club's security. 'I want ecstasy,' I admitted.

'Do you want me to get you some?' Bryan asked, his dark brown eyes a mixture of altruism and horniness.

'Could you do that? That'd be amazing.'

He leaned leftward, away from me, to another bearish man. They chatted for a few seconds and then Bryan leaned back against me. 'Have you got thirty dollars?'

I pulled a twenty and a ten from my wallet and gave them to him. He went diagonal again for a while then straightened. 'Here you go, babe.' His hand went to my crotch, I placed my hand beneath his and a little pill dropped into my palm. I threw it in my mouth and washed it down with beer.

While I waited for paradise to boom through my body, I sat with Bryan, grateful for his help and flattered by his attention.

The ecstasy soon kicked in, just as I remembered. Around the beer garden, clouds of cigarette smoke soared skyward numinously. People's faces shone like angels. The neon signs which I could see inside the club had now taken on a celestial appearance. I ran my fingers over my jeans enjoying the lovely denim texture.

'Your pupils are massive,' Bryan teased, watching me.

'Yes' was the only word I managed to push through my gooey tranquility. I looked at Bryan. He was at least ten years older than the young gays and lesbians babbling and laughing around us in the beer garden. There was something sad in his eyes. I felt he had struggled in life. 'You know you're very handsome,' I told him, searching his round face with its chrome purple eyebrow piercing and coarse brown beard.

'You are,' he giggled, playfully swatting my chest.

I locked eyes with him and we held each other's gaze. He looked down at my lips and back into my eyes, leaned forward and kissed me. It was nice, gentle, devoid of eroticism, like a deeper form of a hug.

'Look at you two,' a woman interrupted. I looked up to see a thin and rough-looking woman with a mohawk who seemed to be a friend of Bryan. 'Who's this?'

'His name is Corey,' Bryan said, proudly placing an arm around me. 'He's a straight boy. Apparently,' he said, this last word between two campy air quotes. 'Corey, this is Lisa.'

I fought against the immobility that now imbued my whole body and said hello.

'You're a bit cute,' she said maternally, lighting a cigarette.

'Isn't he just,' crowed Bryan, kissing me tenderly on my temple.

Bryan and Lisa started talking about a woman Lisa had a crush on, who was due to arrive at the club shortly.

This pill was different to the one I had taken with Nina and Tim, more introspective. It hadn't sparked a wild urge to move my body. I was content to sit, listening to Bryan and Lisa pick apart the dynamics of her feelings for the woman, while the rest of the people in the smoker's area murmured, laughed, shouted or silently kissed and embraced.

I felt I was almost going to fall asleep from the pill, experiencing a brief anxiety that maybe the pill hadn't been ecstasy at all but a date-rape drug. Then the sleepiness evaporated, replaced by a hyperactive need to move my body. I shot up off the bench and announced to Bryan and Lisa that I had to dance. 'Are you going to come with me?'

He shook his head. 'I'm not really a dancer,' he said. He swept his hands downwards over his body to emphasise his point.

'Come on,' I sang. 'Who cares? Dancing is for everyone.'

I skipped away to the deafening swirl of the humid dance floor.

When I felt the pill wearing off hours later, I returned to Bryan still seated in the smoking area and I hit him up for another pill.

'I don't know if you need another pill,' he said in a concerned voice.

'I'm fine,' I said, my teeth chattering, his face blurred at the edges. I grabbed both his hands and pouted at him, puppy dog eyes.

'Hmm,' he hesitated.

I stooped to deliver a lingering kiss on both of his cheeks. 'Pleeeeeeasssseeee.'

'Okay, but no more after this one,' he said gruffly, as I thrust a wad of money at him.

I ate the second pill then skipped back to the dance floor. I danced for ages, sometimes by myself and sometimes with others, swimming in bottomless satisfaction.

The music abruptly cut out and a security guard was bellowing, 'That's it! Time to go home! The night is over!'

The few dozen of us left in the club filed out the entrance and onto the cigarette-littered, chewing-gum-marred pavement. In the early grey sunlight, women with cuts and bruises on their legs held broken high heels and stumbled into traffic. Previously immaculate twinks now looked like they had skin diseases from hours of sweating that had made their spray tans run. Butch lesbians had lost their voices from shouting and now sounded hoarse, on the verge of death. Bryan and I walked past one another, but pretended we hadn't seen each other. Our intimacy had been artificial and did not extend beyond the half-life of ecstasy.

I looked around me. Everybody seemed ghoulish, misshapen, debauched, fallen. I had to get out of there. I hailed a taxi to college and dropped into bed.

I woke up around 7 o'clock that night feeling flat and hollow. Quickly, I showered and headed back to The Beat. I picked up a pill, danced, bought another pill, danced some more.

I began to spend every weekend there. I liked that I could go to The Beat and a dealer might give me a discount on pills if I was coy enough, flirted with him, or pecked him on the cheek. I felt wanted, which I had never been before. And I felt my truest self on ecstasy.

My entire life began to revolve around The Beat. The people there *got it*. Hedonism was celebrated. Libertinism was a mark of coolness. I had been so painfully earnest and sincere for so long that the culture of camp, of irony, gossip and willing embrace of degeneracy, was liberating. The months I'd spent torturing myself over The Answer to the Meaning of Life seemed a lifetime ago. I'd found The Answer: pleasure. What did it matter if God existed, if we persisted beyond death, when we could go out, munted on pills, and dance to Rihanna's 'Umbrella' and Daryl Braithwaite's 'The Horses'?

Had I finally found the place where I belonged? The gay community was full of outsiders like me. For a lot of them, rejected because of who they lusted for, who their hearts leapt into their mouths for, the gay scene was more of a family than their own. In this way, I was with them.

I started to go home with men, to have a man hover above me in the darkness, feel his belly move on mine and his stubble brush my neck, to taste him, to wait with bated breath for where his kisses would drop onto my flesh, to feel him enter me as I hissed in pain that his gentle hips turned to pleasure. I basked in the feeling that someone thought I was worthwhile and beautiful.

I thought I was gay. Hell, I wanted to be gay. It made sense: I had always been awkward around women. It must be because I was gay, right? And I craved solidity, stability. Whose dick did I have to suck around here to feel a stable sense of self?

I gave it my best shot. I kissed them, I jerked them off, I blew them, danced with them at the peak of drugs, took them home and let them fuck me. If one of them fell in love with me, maybe the yawning hollowness inside me could be filled in. Maybe I wouldn't need drugs, which had been so incredible at first, but now became grittier, dirtier, darker.

These experiences always occurred under the influence of drugs, though. When I was sober, I struggled to manifest carnal desire for them. The morning after one-night-stands, I never continued the previous night's sex. Instead I enjoyed the stillness of our two warm bodies beside each other, shifting during sleep.

Men fucked me but they didn't save me. Instead of happily ever after I had loads of cum swung onto my belly by grunting men pulling out of me in the darkness. Nothing lasted except my alienation.

When I wasn't as high as a giraffe in a hot air balloon, I read the Beat writers – Ginsberg, Kerouac and Burroughs – along with Walt Whitman. Their vision of the world as one of adventure, intoxication and romantic grittiness, combined with the mania of the drugs which I now took pretty much around the clock, made me feel that my life, our lives, with their seediness and synthetic intimacy, were holy. I was seeing the best minds of my generation being destroyed by madness. I was living through a time of bloodied beauty. This was important; this was meaningful.

I got a tattoo on my right wrist, *Amor, Veritas, Fortitudo*. Latin for *Love, Truth, Courage*, and English for *Dickhead*.

It was a world of shallowness that I mistook for profundity.

Ecstasy stopped being the illuminating, cleansing substance that it once was, so I went for harder drugs, chasing that initial night of ineffable delight. Ecstasy gave way to LSD gave way to 2C-E and other drugs with names like licence plates.

Drugs drenched my life with significance. Through them I attained transcendence and beautification. It was the romance of stumbling chemically crucified into a lilac dawn. It was peeling a woman's shirt off as she slipped her underwear down her legs and bent over so you could fuck her in the toilet, her panties like soft chains around her calves. It was fucking her in a dirty club bathroom, the tiles echoing your twin moans. It was a sordid magic elevating you out of a busted world. It was filth making things immaculate.

I wanted to smash myself to pieces, to find something fundamental and enduring. This was the revving engine of my delusion. As my drug-taking sequences grew into weeks, as my derangement grew, I'd bail people up in the beer garden at The Beat and preach the importance of self-destruction.

'You cannot understand mathematics without understanding prime numbers, the building blocks of all other numbers,' I sermonised with a scabbed cigarette wobbling in my drug-palsied mouth. 'My theory then is that we must, through drugs and self-annihilation more broadly, reduce ourselves to the prime numbers of our being in order to understand who we are.' At which point my conversation partner would realise I was insane and depart.

I failed every one of my university classes, but didn't care a jot. I moved out of college and in with some friends from The Beat. Things took on a darker turn, less Jack Kerouac, more Irvine Welsh.

One evening, a new scent filled a party. My curiosity piqued, I went to investigate.

'Hey, what are you guys doing?'

'Ice,' my friend Luke replied casually.

'Oh. Can I have some?' I asked.

'Yeah, of course.'

I flopped beside him on the couch. 'So how do I do this?'

'Let me help you,' he said, and held the pipe to my lips. The lighter's flame shot, and he told me to suck in.

Glory. That was the first word that shot into my head as it hit me and my lips fell away from the glass. *Glory.* I slumped back on the couch. *Glory.*

Inhaling the strangely sweet vapour was like breathing in godhood. Suddenly the universe was mine to rule. All things were possible. It made the pleasure of ecstasy feel like being kneed in the balls.

We continued re-dosing through the night, gibbering about nonsense, wide-eyed with limitless energy.

I left the house around noon the next day, trudging along the hot grey Brisbane streets like a graveyard dragging itself through the world. My neck ached so much I couldn't move my chin, and my head was stuck looking slightly upwards at the powerlines dissecting the sky like black scalpels. A surreal, menacing quality infused people, buildings, traffic.

I was utterly depleted. My feet seemed capable only of moving two centimetres at a time. Each time I crossed at a set of traffic lights, cars honked angrily at my sluggishness. Everything was shit, mud and death.

I got home and collapsed into bed, fell into a deep sleep. When I woke it was past midnight – I'd slept for thirteen hours straight, yet felt more exhausted than I'd ever been. I felt like dirty broken glass. Moving an arm or a leg took herculean, agonising effort, as though all my muscles had been replaced by thin wires which sliced and slashed my bones with any motion.

Despite this, my only thought was that I wanted more ice. Every cell in my body screamed for it. I wanted to feel once more that limitless feeling of total possibility of the night before. It now seemed as essential to me as water and air.

I hobbled to the shower at a snail's pace and let the water wash away the poisonous film on my body. I dressed then headed back to The Beat. In the beer garden, I found Harry, a dealer I'd scored ecstasy from a couple of times. I asked if he could get ice.

'You want ice?' he asked, worried.

'Yes,' I snipped, frustrated at being questioned.

'Are you sure?'

'Yes.'

'Okay. Gimme a sec.' He left and returned fifteen minutes later, inviting me to sit down beside him while we went through the theatre of having a cigarette to disguise the transaction.

'Here's a hundred's worth,' he said.

I slyly held the money in my hand at my side, which Harry substituted for a little bag.

'Stay for a bit after I leave then go.' He walked away while I texted Luke to tell him I had a gift he might like to share with me.

We stayed up for days smoking ice and the sunlight was a machine gun as we walked the streets but we were invincible, we were invincible, we were invincible.

'Oh God, I need to shit. Wait there,' I squeaked to Luke, making a beeline for a set of stairs that led to an underground car park.

I tore my sweaty black jeans down to my ankles and dropped into a squat, sighing as the brown slop splattered onto the hot concrete.

Ice made me feel mythological. After all, I was the only human being walking through the CBD in clothes I'd been wearing for days, sweating profusely, mistaking shadows for old women slitting their own throats with knives. I was made worthwhile by what I'd overcome. I burned and blasted myself and it was good. It was noble.

It went on, two- and three- and four-day ice binges followed by up to a week of sleeping. Compared to other drugs I'd done, coming down from ice was especially brutal.

My gums bled. I kept a bucket beside my bed and every ten minutes or so I would spit blood into it. When I managed to finally fall asleep, upon regaining consciousness, I'd find blood had leaked from my mouth onto my pillow, leaving maroon lakes all across it. Or I'd end up swallowing it so that I would wake up and rush to the bathroom with diarrhoea. I hallucinated snake heads on the walls, briefly becoming convinced Dr Phil was in the room with me to conduct an intervention.

Paranoia swelled in me. I would make friends and drop them when I intuited they might be thinking about murdering me.

My impulse control rotted. When a friend cancelled a planned night out with me, I screamed down the phone at him about how he was dead to me. 'Come near me again and I'll kill you! You've betrayed me.' I could feel my face mutate with hate.

None of this bothered me. I was too far gone. There was no golden future any more, nothing to strive for. There was only ice. The only substance in the world that mattered.

Drug addiction granted me a sense of compassion for my mother. Previously, I felt a cool anger towards her for being a drug addict. How could somebody abandon their children for drugs?

The answer, it turned out, was pretty easily. The descent into drugs was an ascent into a kind of heaven and, as with religion, people would sacrifice virtually anything for it.

I recognised the truth of drug addiction: nobody intends it. What begins as innocent pleasure, a brief reprieve from life's problems, metastasises. It conquers you. It's a similar evolution as with watching pornography: it starts out as fun, then you find yourself wanting more, and then a couple of years down the track the only way you can orgasm is by watching women body builders scissoring oak trees.

Understanding this took the sting out of my mother's abandoning me for drugs.

I'd been doing ice for about a year when I nearly died. I didn't suffer a stroke or a heart attack, or receive a beating from a dealer – I nearly choked to death on a potato gem.

I was coming down from a three-day binge and, after seventy-plus hours of grinding and gurning, my jaw no longer functioned. I was essentially a human tapeworm who could still participate in capitalism.

I was staggering home down Brunswick Street when I heard someone say my name. I pivoted to see if it was real or I was imagining it, the latter of which occasionally happened after longer benders.

The voice was not a hallucination. It belonged to Steven, from Nudgee. He still had the same round face and helmet-like haircut, only his puppy fat had been replaced with muscle.

'Oh, hey, Steven,' I said.

I watched him look me up and down. 'Hey, Corey,' he trailed off. I could tell he was shocked by my appearance. An idea formed in my head.

'It's so great to see you,' I said. 'I'm actually on my way home, but say, do you think you could lend me five dollars?'

'Yeah, no worries.' In one smooth motion, Steven reached into his back pocket, grabbed his wallet and rifled through it. 'Have ten dollars, mate,' he said, gentler than he'd ever been at school.

'Thanks, mate. I'll definitely pay you back next time I see you. I promise.' I excused myself and ducked into a pizza shop down the street, where I ordered a large bowl of potato gems. I hadn't eaten for days and my stomach sounded like an Aphex Twin song.

My jaw aching, I was forced to swallow the hot potato pieces whole, unchewed, like a seal. Then one lodged in my throat, and, even after thirty seconds of choking and beating my own chest, it wouldn't leave.

Sitting beside me was a middle-aged man reading a newspaper. I banged the table with my hands. He cast a sidelong glance at me. I pointed at my throat, miming a Heimlich manoeuvre on myself in the most high-stakes game of charades of my life. His eyes blew wide in understanding. He rocketed backwards on his chair with a screech and sped to my side. Then he spun me around and embraced me from behind, wrapping his arms around me, locking his hands together and squeezing.

Unfortunately, he wasn't performing the procedure correctly. Instead of pumping my stomach, his arms were up further, around my chest. My field of vision grew inky like water around a dying squid. Regions of space turned black. I clutched at his arms desperately, trying to reposition them.

Finally the potato gem shot out of my mouth and landed on the table. I sucked greedily at the air while the man patted me on the shoulder. When I'd regained my breath, I thanked him profusely and offered to pay for his meal. He declined, which was fortunate because I didn't have any more money. If he'd accepted, I would have had to do a runner on this Good Samaritan. Making sure I was okay one last time, my hero returned to his table. Then I caught the train home and collapsed in bed.

Lying there, I knew I had to quit ice. The slow disintegration of my mental and physical health hadn't bothered me. Rubbing shoulders with criminals and borderline-insane people hadn't bothered me. But now it had affected my ability to eat potato gems.

It was a bizarre way to terminate an addiction to drugs, but on reflection it makes sense.

It didn't happen immediately, of course. To make sure I wasn't making a rash decision, I did ice a few more times, but I couldn't shake the gnawing anxiety that something would go wrong.

Eventually, I kicked ice by replacing it with alcohol because life isn't a fairytale.

10

I cut ties with everyone from The Beat and, wanting to create an entirely new life, I started looking for work. There was no other way to be clean. It had to be all-or-nothing. With no skills, minimal experience and incomplete higher education, though, my options were limited to temp contracts in call centres.

It was brainless and soul-destroying work. For eight hours a day, I'd sit under fluorescent lighting repeating the same script two hundred times to the voices on the other end of the line. After each shift I'd practically sprint to the nearest bar and drink like a lab rat pressing a cocaine pedal.

I knew it was better to be clean but I was lost in my cleanness. I couldn't see a way forward, and I wanted somebody to save me. I'd sit in pubs until midnight and look at a woman and think, *Could she be my soulmate?* I'd wonder if a barfly might become a father figure to me. Sometimes, when I was very drunk, I'd be seized by the mad hope that my mother would walk into the bar.

Something was missing in me. Other people seemed so *solid*, while I felt like an empty birdcage. Without study or drugs to distract me, I tried to fill the hollowness with affectations and hobbies and habits that would make me real. I underwent so many phases in a bid to find an identity.

For a while, I went to strip clubs, trying to be a degenerate. I'd go in after work and pay for a lap dance, lean back as strippers sashayed over to grind upon me and lightly massage my face with their breasts cool from the air-conditioning like the unused side of a pillow. After months of this, though, I was as lost as ever and so changed tack again.

There was the Hunter S. Thompson phase wherein I wrote political essays with self-consciously edgy titles such as *Kevin Rudd Must Eat His Mother's Forearms for the Commonwealth to Prosper* and *Give Me Euthanasia or Give Me Death: Potshots From a Drunken Madman*.

There was my Bukowski phase, the terrible scourge of so many twenty-something men. I wrote awful poetry like

poetry is mostly read by poets.
it's like we're all staring into
each other's assholes
and saying how good
each other's shit is.

that's some nice shit
you got there.

you too, man, you
too.

———

These attempts at being somebody always floundered. My sense of having no identity grew. I felt like a void unperson playing at being a human. A fatter, more timid Patrick Bateman. I couldn't escape the conviction that something fundamental to being human had been mangled in me early on, leaving a zero where a soul should be.

I started drinking heavily, running twenty-five hangovers a month. I ballooned out to 110 kilograms. Until I stopped looking in the mirror, I'd catch a sight of my bloated gut adorned with a belt of red stretch marks, like Rambo wearing a vest of bad choices instead of bullets. If there were a way to convert self-hatred into energy, I could have powered the whole world.

I used alcohol to delete everything in my head. On waking from a bender I felt as though my mental slate had been wiped clean. I began each day anew, disconnected from the chain of days before it. Hangovers narrowed my life to one goal: survive the brutal hangover during a day of work, at the end of which I could get drunk again and repeat the cycle. My life became nothing outside waking up hungover, working at the call centre and going to sleep drunk, comfortable margins that didn't permit sinking too deeply into myself.

One boozy night I was at Chalk Hotel in Brisbane, annihilating jugs of beer, trying to erase consciousness. I stumbled into the male toilets to make room for more alcohol in my bladder. There was a hulk pissing into a urinal. The cubicle was occupied, which forced me to go to plan B of sidling up beside him.

'Brpf,' he burped, swaying towards me.

'Sorry?'

'BRPF!' he snarled, tottering closer.

I stepped to the side. 'Sorry?'

Suddenly he seized my throat and slammed me against the tiled wall above the urinal. 'Brpf,' he shouted into my face like a belligerent stroke survivor. I saw his shoulder pull back and felt him punch me in the stomach, my breath whooshing out like a leaf blower. 'Brpf!' the goon grunted angrily. He caught me with another punch to the gut, only this time it wasn't air that shot out of my mouth. Instead, an amber prism of beer and potato wedges shot out of my mouth and engulfed his head. He screamed and dropped to his knees, pawing the sick from his eyes. For the first time in our brief relationship he spoke English: 'Cunt!'

I legged it out of the toilets and hailed a cab.

So, in a way, alcohol saved my life.

An old chess acquaintance contacted me out of the blue on Myspace. I told him about getting clean and trying to go straight. He'd started doing stand-up comedy and encouraged me to try my hand at it. I'd never harboured any desire to be a comedian, but I took him up on the offer – here, perhaps, was another identity to try on. I wrote a five-minute set and a fortnight later I performed my first open mic. The set received only scattered chuckles but these thrilled me no end.

I decided to stick with it. I hadn't 'found myself' onstage or anything as cloying as that. Comedy just seemed a nice fit for my problems, not unlike a short man discovering he can be a jockey. And I was spending my nights getting drunk in pubs anyway, I might as well try comedy.

Plus it kept me busy and my mind off drugs, which at the time was all I could think about. I missed how drugs rescued me from the mundanity of life and rendered everything silken and lucid. And even though I felt desolate coming down from ice, it was at least briefer than the grinding banality of call centres. Until stand-up comedy became part of my life, I'd been teetering on the edge of resuming drugs.

I devoured comedy albums and DVDs. I listened to podcasts in the shower, on public transport, during lunch, in the toilet at work. I wrote ceaselessly, poring over my jokes to strip all the fat from them, searching for ways to shrink the distance between set-up and punchline. Comedy is brevity. Humour is snappy. It's about getting rid of all the extraneous detail and zeroing in on one feature alone. It's a kind of mathematics, which appealed to me. My jokes became gems of logic, diamonds of surprise.

I struck up genuine friendships with other comedians. They were interesting, witty and often depressed, a trifecta of traits that put me at ease.

A friend, Alex, once said that the gods made the Brisbane comedy world to train the faithful. It was a tough scene, said to be the toughest in the country, especially for those of us new to comedy. To be a comedian was to be a part of this club. A poor, desperate, narcissistic club, but still a club. We were in it together. We killed, we bombed, we did okay. We called non-comedians civilians and ourselves fat cunts.

Most of us were in our late teens and early twenties and we despised the older middle-aged comedians who worked the better clubs. As new comedians, we gigged exclusively in low-level, sparsely attended venues. Occasionally, we even performed in bars with no audience members, continuing only because of contractual obligations and the chance people might wander in.

If we impressed at these dive bar gigs we were given opportunities to perform in proper comedy clubs. While paid, they came with their own set of challenges, namely hens parties in the audience wearing dildos on their heads, heckling and screaming at random intervals, which convinced me that marriage was a toxic, patriarchal institution that should be abolished. Bucks parties of swaggering men who were liable to launch into violence over imagined slights drove me to sympathise with radical feminists from the 1970s who called for the male population to be culled down to a few breeding studs kept in muddy cages.

Nothing beat killing on stage, regaling a roomful of strangers. The rush of endorphins following a good gig, while unable to compare with the sheer splendour of ice, did feel earned, and it didn't result in my gums bleeding for a week afterwards, and strangers weren't frightened of me after I'd done it.

Conversely, nothing was worse than bombing on stage. Few things could compare to the ego-melting shame of standing in front of a room full of silent strangers who had watched me with the expectation I'd have them rolling in the aisles. Parents had hired babysitters to listen to me mumble unfunnily about my arsehole. Under the glare of a harsh spotlight, I'd have an out-of-body experience watching words tumble out of the dry mouth of a moron. When I finished and slunk into the shadows, I wanted to feed myself to a pit bull.

I loved it all. Everything added up to an exciting, surprising life of self-expression.

I loved that in stand-up you could say anything. All conceivable topics were ripe for laughs. You didn't even need the audience to laugh if you were happy to bomb. It was 2008 and nothing was off limits. It was a different time. Twitter was still new and outrage had not yet started to outsell sex. And it didn't hurt that it was Brisbane, regarded as a provincial outpost unimportant to Australian show business. You were allowed to make mistakes, to fail, fall, fuck up. It was the perfect environment for comedy. We flourished – macho everyman comics, oddball surrealists and hard-nosed satirists alike.

Over the next two years, my act evolved from absurd one-liners into more politically charged rants. Bill Hicks made a strong impression on me and I consciously imitated him, adopting his 'truth teller' persona, which in my hands mostly involved screaming about smoking laws at electricians nibbling on potato wedges. I would 'punch up' with analogies between queefs and drone strikes. Yes, I was the lone brave voice daring to say that 'racism is bad'. I was a self-righteous dunce.

Gradually I accumulated the experiences every comedian does: levelling a room with laughter, bombing, being heckled, getting too drunk before a gig, Australian soldiers wanting to bash you to death for off-colour jokes about the armed forces.

The latter, terrifying event occurred in the wake of a set I performed about how war was bad – brave, iconoclastic stuff. I was twenty-one and in another one of my phases, this time libertarianism. I was all about personal freedom and small government, convictions that heavily informed my comedy at the time, providing an endless supply of contrarian material. I kicked off my set with some nice, accessible pro-consensual adult incest material.

'People say incest is wrong because if they have a baby it'll have birth defects.' I strutted around the stage, absorbing the audience's shock at the topic. 'That's true but, y'know, incest fuckers could just wear a condom! There, solved your problem. But also, who says birth defects are necessarily a bad thing? I mean, evolution only happens because of mutations in our genetic code. That's how our ancestors got thumbs way back in the day, right? Maybe incest babies are how we reach the next stage of human civilisation! Maybe a brother and a sister fuck and they make a big balloon-head mutant baby who can fly.' To emphasise my maverick and fearless point I bobbed and dipped around the stage like said balloon-head baby. A few people cackled, most didn't, a lack of laughter I chalked up to the audience being filled with cowardly conformists.

Believing incorrectly that I was on a roll, I moved onto a new topic without a skerrick of a segue. 'Can someone explain to me why we commemorate Gallipoli?' I ranted, the audience collectively taking a jagged breath. 'I mean, the Anzacs invaded Turkey, a country that never threatened us, and we got our arses handed to us. People say, "Oh, they were conscripted." But they weren't. They *chose* to go. They didn't die fighting for freedom. They died because they were *retards*.'

There was a stony silence. After a couple of seconds, a few people laughed at the silence. I looked out at the audience, and thought to myself that a prophet is never revered in his time.

'Anyway, that's all I've got time for. I've been Corey White. Thanks!' I dashed offstage, satisfied that, while I hadn't been funny, I'd told the audience 'how it was'. The MC announced a fifteen-minute interval and I went to sit down with the other comics, who avoided eye contact with me.

As I drained the dregs of my beer, Jason, a massive unit who did sound for the gig, sidled up beside me. 'Corey,' he said in a low, urgent voice, 'you need to go home. There's a bunch of soldiers here who hated the Anzac stuff. They want to murder you. You have to leave now.'

'It's a free country,' I protested. 'In fact, the Anzacs died fighting for my freedom to criticise them.'

'Man, those dudes are not on the same page as you.'

Jason was quite a relaxed guy so for him to be concerned sent a hot prickling down my neck. I looked over and noticed a half-dozen men with buzz cuts scowling and shaking their heads at me from their seats across the room, while off to the side a woman was restraining another man who'd also failed to appreciate the satirical power of my routine. I watched as the woman's planted legs skidded backwards from his slow, furious march towards me.

Jason called for a taxi on his mobile as he escorted me to the car park, pushing me into the front seat when it arrived, slapping the roof for the driver to make a speedy getaway.

Sometimes comedy turned me into a nasty person. I derived joy from pooping other people's parties. I was jealous of their ability to connect with others, to be happy, because I was fucking miserable and comedy gave me a platform to express that.

I became angrier and angrier on stage, screaming into the microphone about freedom, drunk on beer and my own sense of heroism.

I wasn't naive enough to think that laughter would be some kind of medicine for me. If it was, it was like diabetes medication, curing nothing, merely managing the symptoms of the horror of existence.

As I entered the Happy High Herbs store, I was assaulted by a wave of patchouli, the hippy answer to Lynx deodorant. Its wet-soil smell was the perfect accompaniment for the bullshit New Age products inside. One corner of the tiny purple-walled shop was devoted entirely to hemp products. There were hemp vests, hemp pants, hemp fedoras, hemp wallets, hemp sunglasses, hemp colostomy bags. Another section contained a rack of shirts bearing slogans such as 'Looks Like Barbie, Smokes Like Marley' and 'Not Gonna Lie, Wanna Get High'. On a shelf in another corner sat book-shaped garbage with titles ranging from *Don't Think Like a Human* to *Menopausal Years: The Wise Woman Way*.

A white guy with dreadlocks stood at the counter. 'Brother!' he cried. 'Welcome! What brings you here to this shop out of all the shops in the world?'

'I'm just looking to trip a little bit,' I said.

I was working a temp job in a call centre for the Australian Taxation Office, a role that consisted entirely of updating people's addresses. Any other request was beyond my ken and warranted a transfer to another department. I spent each day having the same phone call with slight variations.

'Welcome to the Australian Taxation Office, this is Corey speaking. How may I help you?'

'I'd like someone to explain why I've been taxed so highly for the last financial quarter since the year before that I filed for bankruptcy and bought a second-hand car with money I inherited from my grandmother who I cared for over two tormenting years. She had bowel cancer and dementia, because the world is pain. Now I get a letter from you lizards saying I've got a tax debt of three grand. I can't handle this stress, this is criminal.'

'Sir, unfortunately I'm only trained to update your address. I'll just transfer you to the correct section,' I'd say then dial the right department's number and hit the transfer button. The line would go silent for a moment before a *BEEP* announced a new customer.

'Welcome to the Australian Taxation Office, this is Corey speaking. How may I help you?'

'Listen here, you little cat-drowning bureaucrat, I want to know why I'm being asked to pay money to the Tax Office.'

'Sir, unfortunately I'm only trained to update your address. I'll just transfer you to the correct section.'

BEEP.

'Welcome to the Australian Taxation Office, this is Corey speaking. How may I help you?'

'I'd just like to update my address, please.'

'I can certainly assist you with that . . . Madam, unfortunately it seems my computer is encountering technical difficulties. I apologise for this but I'll just need to transfer you to a colleague.'

My right index finger had developed a callus from transferring calls. It was trivial work they could have trained a chimp to do.

I craved something approaching the liberating beauty of LSD. And since the fine print on my vow to stay off drugs didn't mention *legal* ones, I'd trudged into Happy High Herbs looking for a substance that might fit that loophole.

'Brother!' the shop assistant exclaimed. 'I can help! Sometimes we all need a break from reality!' I felt confident he could assist me. If the rancid stench from his armpits was anything to go by, he was an expert on eluding reality.

Vanilla Bob Marley downward-dogged underneath the counter. Reappearing, he dumped a box in front of me. Inside was a smorgasbord of pills, powders, seeds and liquids. Above it, his locks shuddered as he launched into a sales pitch.

'This little white powder's called "Wicked". It's the strongest legal high on the market and so far has escaped any and all bans. This little fella here is the Californian poppy, closely related to the opium poppy, one of my personal favourites.'

He looked like a free spirit but spoke like a vacuum salesman. On and on he went, pimping products until my snapping patience drove me at last to settle on some Hawaiian baby woodrose seeds.

'Ah! Excellent choice, good sir. That'll be forty-five dollars.' I handed over the money. 'Aloha,' he said, with a shit-eating grin.

My housemates weren't home. I took the seeds from the packet and examined them. Each was the size of a ball bearing, hard and grey-brown. I swallowed three with some water and lay down in bed.

Nothing happened.

I looked at the light of my bedside lamp hoping for even mild visual distortions.

Nothing.

After thirty minutes, the only feeling I had was of being duped. I'd been ripped off yet again. I'd been ripped off countless times. It felt as if I'd been ripped off in an infinity of previous lives. I had been ripped off by that same man in the store throughout eternity and would continue to be ripped off by him in countless future lives too. My whole life had been repeated numerous times and would be repeated countless more, and in each life I was ripped off.

The Hawaiian baby woodrose seeds were working a treat but I couldn't tell.

My mobile phone rang, as it had rung a trillion times before. I leaned over to my eternal bedside drawer and picked up my ever-lasting Nokia 3310.

It was my friend John. 'Hey man, I just wanted to pick up that book I lent you.'

'Oh yes,' I said for the umpteenth time in this and every lifetime.

I met John at my front door and handed him the book, deja vu like a tsunami. *Ahh, deja vu*, I thought, *I remember you.*

The next thing I knew I was lying down in bed yelling, 'Yeehaw!' into the night, over and over. Then I was taking a pane of glass out of a window and biting it, yelling, 'Yeehaw!' Then I was throwing a bottle of wine at a wall. Then I was sitting on the toilet and yelling, 'Yeehaw!'

I came to in bed. It was night-time. There were no lights on in the house. How long had I been out?

My stomach was the *Titanic*. Something was wrong.

Horror exploded within me as I realised I was naked and covered in blood and shit. I tried to recall getting to bed. Flashes of the night's events arose in my mind. Buying the seeds. Swallowing them. John calling to ask for his book back. Meeting John at the door. But what happened after that? Where had John gone?

I thought, *Did I kill John?* I'd killed John. I had murdered my friend.

My mouth was caked with a strange substance, conclusive proof I'd cannibalised him. As I reflected on my newfound status as a man-eater, I heard the front door being unlocked. I poked my head out of my room and saw my housemate Patrick stomping down the hallway. He stopped when he saw me.

'Patrick, I think I've done something bad.'

He padded towards me slowly. 'It's okay, mate,' he said gently. 'How about we get you to put on some clothes while I call an ambulance?'

'Sorry about the blood and shit,' I said, stepping into a pair of boxer shorts and throwing on a t-shirt.

As Patrick talked on the phone in the kitchen, I wandered out to our driveway. The street was silent but I knew that any minute now the cops would be coming to arrest me. I scanned the night sky for police helicopters. There were none. I looked at the roofs of the houses in the street. There could be sharpshooters ready to take me down. Yes, I had murdered John, but that was because of the drugs. Didn't they realise I wasn't a threat? What if they thought I'd taken Patrick hostage? I lay belly down on the concrete and yelled out, 'I don't have any weapons! Please don't kill me!' I had decided my chances of survival hinged on politeness. I needed to prove the cannibalistic rage was a blip in the history of a good boy.

An ambulance arrived and Patrick spoke with the paramedics. I remained face down on the concrete, trying to look as meek as possible. Starting now, I would be an exemplary prisoner in the hope a parole board would shave a few months off my sentence down the line.

'It says here you murdered your best friend and ate his intestines,' they'd say. 'But since that awful act you've been incredibly well-mannered. It is this board's opinion you are fit to re-enter society.'

'Thank you,' I'd say from the bottom of a deep bow.

I wasn't sure how I would survive prison. What I would have to do was pull some stunt to either get people to leave me alone or have me transferred to the special ward they have for police and paedophiles. It would probably have to involve a great deal of violence, which was at odds with my politeness strategy. *Fuck. My life is ruined.*

'Hi Corey, do you want to come with us to the hospital?' I looked up from the concrete like a naughty dog. A female paramedic was leaning down with a kind, open face. I stood up cautiously and allowed her to shepherd me into the moonlit ambulance and onto a stretcher.

I spotted Patrick in the driveway. Thinking of my looming court case, I shouted, 'Tell the police I didn't take hostages!' I was going to need all the brownie points I could get.

As we drove off, a worm of vanity came to me. I leaned over to the paramedic sitting with me. 'Hey, am I missing teeth?'

'Show me,' she said. I opened my mouth. 'No, they're all there.'

'You can be honest with me,' I whispered for no reason, 'I don't have any teeth, do I?'

'You have all your teeth.'

I could tell she was lying, but I played along. I had to think of the court case. She might end up being a character witness. 'Thank you for being honest with me,' I said.

As we drove to the hospital, I thought about how my toothlessness would affect the court case. I pictured the jurors averting their eyes when I took the stand to testify, wincing as my mouth-hole made strange sucking sounds. They would, of course, find me guilty. The judge, too, would be repulsed, and would impose the harshest sentence.

I closed my eyes against the harsh lighting of the ambulance. I had murdered my friend and eaten him and lost all my teeth. I could taste bits of him in my mouth. Grim questions assailed me. How much had I eaten of him? Which parts? I couldn't shake the feeling I had munched on his eyeball.

I felt the ambulance become motionless. The doors swung outwards and I was guided off the stretcher and down to the bitumen expanse of a hangar. The paramedic led me through a set of sliding doors into the hospital. I looked around for police officers but none had arrived yet.

'Excuse me,' I asked, as we rounded a turn. 'Where are the police?'

The paramedic didn't respond.

We came to a small, painfully white waiting room. The paramedic sat down beside me on a chair. I felt a pain in my bladder.

'Can I use the toilet?' I asked.

'Yeah, sure. It's just over there,' she said, pointing to a door a few metres away.

For the first time I entered a bathroom as a murderer. I strode to the urinal and pulled out my dick. When I finally started pissing it was pure yellow, like the Velvet Underground banana. I finished up and spun around, catching a glimpse of myself in the mirror. There was no blood or shit. I opened my mouth and my teeth were all in place. I ran my fingers over them to confirm. Why had I thought my teeth were gone?

Then it hit me. This was a dream. I looked around at the toothpaste-commercial white of the hospital bathroom. A sense of unreality pervaded it all. I must have fallen asleep after taking the Hawaiian baby woodrose seeds. I wasn't a murderer, haha! I wasn't a cannibal, hooray! John was still alive, with an unbitten face. I positively skipped out of the bathroom and took my seat beside the paramedic.

Wonder replaced shame and fear as my head hummed with the possibilities of my lucid dream. I had read a little about lucid dreaming. I knew that people used it to achieve self-realisation and secure stunning insights that transformed their lives. They could control the events of their lucid dream, shape its narrative, environment and characters at will. I closed my eyes and focused on turning the hospital waiting room into a park with beautiful green grass. I opened my eyes. Nope, still the drab waiting room. I thought maybe I had to co-operate with the people in my dream. I asked the female paramedic sitting next to me if we could go to a park. She said no, I had to go to the emergency room, but maybe I could go to a park after. I asked her what would happen if I just went to the park. She told me security would return me to the hospital.

'Well,' I said. 'This is a very authoritarian dream.'

A pretty nurse appeared in front of me. 'Corey, could you come this way with me?'

'It would be my absolute pleasure,' I fawned, desperate to get to the park.

We walked through corridors before emerging into a noisy ward. A sign on the wall read EMERGENCY. The nurse escorted me into a curtained-off part of the chaos. Peeling back the sheets of a metal hospital bed, she patted the mattress for me. I hopped in and pulled the blankets up to my chin.

'Don't get too comfortable. I need your arm,' she said. I offered it to her. She needed to attach some tubes to me, a needle would be required. 'This might hurt,' she said.

'It's okay, this is all a dream. But you're very sweet.'

The nurse left when she was done and I lay there astonished at how real the pain had seemed.

The curtain around my patch of the ER ward bulged, birthing a young, handsome doctor holding a clipboard. He closed the curtain before coming over to me.

'Hello, Mr White.'

'Hello, doctor.'

'Corey, are you by any chance a comedian?'

'Uh, yeah.'

'I thought so. I saw you perform at Newmarket Hotel last week. You were very funny. I loved your bit about the nanny state.'

I was now convinced I was dreaming: a doctor complimenting my stand-up couldn't be real. It had to be vanity, a project of my ego.

'So,' the doctor went on, 'the nurse tells me you've taken some drugs. What kind?'

'Hawaiian baby woodrose seeds.'

'Okay. And you're not feeling very well?'

I looked at the doctor's face. He had blond hair and blue eyes. Clearly he was an archetype. 'Listen, *doctor*. This is a dream. I don't know if you know that but I do. You're an aspect of myself.'

'Sure,' he said, and scribbled something on a paper pad.

'So,' I continued, 'what is something I should know to be a better person?'

'That'll be all for now,' he replied, disappearing through a swirling of the baby-blue hospital curtain. He didn't return.

'I'm trying to work out what this dream means,' I told the nurse as I swallowed the pill she handed me. 'Can you tell me how I escape this?' She disappeared and I pondered what her disappearance signified. It seemed that whenever I mentioned the dream to people in the dream they were hesitant to assist.

I listened to the hubbub of the ER, eager to find insights about myself in the conversations of the patients and staff who were my creations. An old man in the bed beside me complained about Asians and diabetes. Somewhere out to the left of my bed an unseen woman was wailing. None of it seemed to make sense. I couldn't harvest any epiphanies from the chaos. But perhaps that was the point? That there was no truth to cling to, that I should remember it was absurd to encompass everything in a neat set of beliefs.

I lay in the bed and waited. And waited. In a frozen eternity I waited.

A nurse informed me I was being moved to the emergency psychiatric ward, and off we went. When we arrived I took a seat in the reception area. Why, I wondered, had my unconscious chosen a psychiatric ward as the dream setting? Was this a commentary on my own fear of going crazy? Maybe there was no point in trying to make sense of this dream.

A young woman was admitted and sat across from me. She was slender, pale and young, with black hair and brown eyes. Her thin arms were covered with scars, macramé the colour of watermelon. She was lean with delicate legs in black skinny jeans, a shapely void against the speckled hospital linoleum. My dick stirred through the thin fabric of my gingham boxers and I thought about fucking her. I had always wanted to have sex in a dream. I thought, *Where would*

we have sex? Right here in the ward? What if she doesn't want to fuck me?
I considered the morality of dream rape before concluding that, even
in dreams, rape is wrong.

Her eyes met mine. 'Stop looking at me, you fucking weirdo.'

My erection wilted. 'You're not real,' I said petulantly.

After our clash, we sat in silence for what felt like hours. I had
given up on the notion of time in the dream. A nurse came out with
a pill in one hand and a plastic cup of water in the other. 'Take this,
please.' I held out my hand and she dropped the white tablet into
my palm. I tossed it into my mouth and drank the water, recalling
swallowing the seeds. The nurse left with the cup.

I woke up and, with a sinking feeling, realised I was still in the
hospital. When would this goddamn dream end? My neck burned.
'I want to fucking wake up!' I growled at the ceiling, trying to awaken
my conscious mind.

I pictured my housemates trying to wake me up in real life.
'Corey!' they'd say, swatting me with exponential panic. That
wouldn't work so they'd tip buckets of water over me, also to no avail.
Then they would look helplessly at each other and together stare
perplexed at my wet Sleeping Beauty body. They'd call an ambulance,
which would drive me to the hospital, and I would spend my whole
life in a coma, developing bedsores on the backs of my neck and
knees. Life in the dream would go on. It would become so boring.
How could I escape it? I considered bashing my head against the
wall until I saw my bedroom. But what if that killed me in real life

too? I wished I'd read more about lucid dreaming. I realised bitterly that the Happy High Herbs store probably had a book on the subject.

A nurse interrupted my reverie. 'Good morning,' she said, setting a tray of food down on the bedside table and leaving. I glanced at it. I couldn't see the point of eating in a dream. Then I noticed the jelly. Since I was on a diet in my waking life, I jumped at the opportunity for a cheat treat. Feeling like an oil company executive after finding a loophole in environmental legislation, I shovelled the red wobbling slime into my mouth. It was delicious. It tasted just like jelly. I felt proud that my subconscious mind could so convincingly ape reality. There was an apple on the tray too but I left it untouched. Why eat healthy snacks in a dream?

After eating, I made my way to the reception area again. I walked up to the receptionist at her booth.

'Can I read the newspaper, please?' I thought my subconscious mind might include a clue in it about how to escape the dream. Possibly in the horoscopes section.

'We don't have a newspaper here,' she replied without looking at me.

Well played, subconscious me, well played.

I sat down on a grey chair. *What if I try to go back to sleep? Maybe I have to sleep twice to wake up.*

I padded back to the nurse once more. 'Hello there. May I go back to sleep please?'

'No,' she said, still looking at her computer screen. 'Patients need to be active.'

I took her injunction to be active and lack of eye contact as a message from my subconscious self that I needed to keep looking for a way out of the dream.

They moved me from the emergency psych ward into the general psych ward, exchanging one sterility for another. It didn't have the disinfectant smell of a hospital. It smelled like nothing. A big white nothing. You never smell in dreams.

'Here's your room,' the orderly said, pushing a door open and revealing a tiny cube, barely large enough for a single bed. The walls were a claustrophobic white and the only natural light came from a rectangle of glass the size of a cricket bat.

'Thank you.' The orderly departed and I closed the door and lay down.

Slowly, I emerged from psychosis. With each Risperidone tablet the nurses fed me, the ward shed a little more of its dreamy skin, assuming the hardness of reality. Events, nurses and patients ceased to have anything to do with the mystical. They had become ordinary. The psychiatric ward was only a psychiatric ward.

I kicked myself because it had been a legal drug. I had made the choice to get the Hawaiian baby woodrose seeds because they were available in a business that paid tax. I'd never had a bad trip on LSD or mushrooms or 2C-B. I resolved to never again do legal drugs. No drug dealer I used from now on would have an ABN.

———

I was surprised the ward wasn't like the one in *One Flew Over the Cuckoo's Nest*. There was no group therapy, no Nurse Ratched savage with power. Mostly we were left to our own devices. We pottered about and slept off the anti-psychotics, made hot chocolate and smoked cigarettes. The banality of our insanity was shocking to me. We had all been broken in some fundamental way, suffered an elemental trauma, yet we were cooped up in this sparse hospital ward scoffing Monte Carlo biscuits. Nobody seemed to recognise the magnitude of what had happened. We were shattered beings with splintered psyches.

One night I realised the door to my room didn't lock. Here I was, in a psychiatric ward, with a door that didn't lock. What if one of these crazy people decided to murder me in my sleep? This was how I knew I had resumed sanity. Fledgling recognition that I was in a psychiatric facility with profoundly mentally unwell people. I spent the next few nights sleeplessly watching my door for intruders wielding plastic sporks or a styrofoam cup of Zippo-heated water. Exhausted by morning, I'd spend the day napping, fingers crossed the schizophrenics, like me, believed daytime murders were uncivilised, a violation of some inviolable social contract.

I was surrounded by people untethered from consensus reality, infected with bizarre ideas about the world, each in his or her own personal parallel universe. How long would I be here? What if I was stuck in this ward for a decade? Fortunately, I soon discovered the silver lining of an underfunded mental health care system is that they're desperate to get you out. First they discharged Terry, despite his confiding to me the morning of his release that he was frightened of getting a computer virus. 'What if my software malfunctions and I kill somebody? Will they upgrade my software or will they just terminate me?'

Next they released Maggie, a lank-haired woman in her mid-thirties with postnatal depression. I'd only spoken to her a few times. I'd made the mistake of joking to her that I also had postnatal depression, because I was depressed that I'd been born. She glowered at me. I continued with a Hail Mary quip. 'You know when my mother was pregnant with me, I spent nine months in the foetal position.' She didn't find that funny either and we didn't speak again, not even when her husband came to pick her up.

At last it was my turn to be set free. 'Corey,' spoke a voice. I glanced up from the TV to see a nurse who gestured for me to follow her. 'The psychiatrist wants to talk to you.'

He asked me, 'How are you feeling today, Corey?'

'Well, much better. I know I'm not dreaming.' I looked into his eyes then at the floor. I was unsure of the correct amount of eye contact to best signal sanity.

I must have got it right because he said, 'Good. Excellent.' He paused, then, in a paternal voice, continued, 'You won't be taking drugs again now, will you?'

I performed the laugh of a sane person. I, too, was a proud citizen of rationality. If there had been a national anthem for sanity I would have stood and sung its lyrics, hand over heart, perfectly balanced between too little affect and too much enthusiasm. I would happily swear an oath to say no to drugs and yes to Euclidean geometry.

'I'm done with drugs. This experience has been a warning. I'm lucky it wasn't worse.'

We spoke a little more, then he slapped the knees of his navy chinos and said, 'Wonderful. Let's get you home, Corey.'

'That's it? I can go?' The situation had the suddenness of a trick.

'Yep,' he said, standing up and walking past me to the door. 'Shall we get somebody to come pick you up?'

Gratitude gushing through my chest, I rose and spoke to his empty chair. 'Sounds dandy.'

After I left the psychiatric ward, I lived in terror of becoming psychotic again. What if I pulled down my pants on a bus and defecated while screaming for world peace? What if I took an elderly woman hostage because I disliked the colour of the sky?

At night, I lay in the same bed where it had all begun, monitoring my mind like a drone, scanning it for any murderous conspiracy. I stopped seeing friends or doing comedy for about six months, so consumed was I with the terror of cannibalising them and being found naked on a roundabout with their stomach in my stomach, wearing their faces as bonnets.

I now worried about other people going crazy too. It had been so easy for me to slip into madness; why not them? Strangers too could be blinded by a false seeing. A bus driver could believe he was Jesus and drive into a crowd of people to trigger the Rapture. He would be mad, but his madness would carry an internal logic as beguiling as mine had been. Now when I waited at a bus stop I stood as far back from the road as possible, legs planted solidly, ready to leap like a soccer goalie, in case my bus was driven by just such a nutter.

Psychosis stained my mind as nicotine stains the fingers. I fell into mental quicksand, playing out the events, scrabbling to find some moment where I might have halted it. Could I have stopped my decline into irrationality? No matter how many times I replayed events, I couldn't get around the fact that they felt normal at the time. Delusion had clicked into delusion, easily, irresistibly.

It was a frightening conclusion. There would be no way of knowing if I was becoming mad again.

On the worst nights, I'd be plagued by a fear that I was still in the psychiatric ward. That I was never discharged but had only sunk deeper into psychosis and, cocooned in lunacy, had imagined all things since, hallucinated leaving the ward, returning to the call centre, everything.

During lunch breaks at work, I'd bite into a sushi roll and wonder if in a higher, more real world I was biting an orderly's thumb; when I folded washing, I was haunted by the possibility that it mapped onto some atrocity outside of my delusion like strangling a psychiatrist.

The scariest thing was that I couldn't completely dismiss the possibility that what I thought had been my life since was imagined. I tried to reassure myself. *Well, I also can't prove that I don't live in a computer simulation constructed by aliens or some variant of* The Truman Show, but the fear remained. How could I ever trust my own mind again?

Anxiety made time flow more slowly, months like honey over a knife, the hellish corollary of the maxim that time flies when you're having fun. For a long time, I tried not to think. I was frightened of my head, scared of what it could do.

I lived seesawing between faith that everything would be okay and despair that I'd snap and wear someone's baby as a shoe. Sometimes I told myself I had to believe I was sane, that believing I was going crazy was a self-fulfilling prophecy. Other times, exhausted from forced hopefulness, I'd be certain of imminent catastrophe. On at least a half dozen occasions I'd catch a taxi to hospital late at night in a fit of panic.

'I think I'm going crazy,' I'd gasp to the nurse at the desk, sweat trickling off my earlobes.

'Okay,' they'd coo bureaucratically. 'Please take a seat.'

I'd slump on an uncomfortable chair, depleted from the effort of not demanding a straitjacket for the good of the other people waiting. I'd pant and sit for a few hours, watching the television, waiting to believe the news would transmit some malevolent instruction which I'd be compelled to follow. Invariably, a wet-behind-the-ears med-student psychiatrist would saunter out, run through my symptoms, look at my file, tell me I was having a panic attack, then send me off with a prescription for Valium.

While I don't recall the exact moment I moved past the trauma of those days of derangement, I know it wasn't a conscious choice. The flight into madness isn't an act of volition and neither is the journey out. Nobody writes 'spiral into insanity' on their bucket list. They just go insane.

In time, my anxiety about becoming psychotic again diminished and was replaced by my old depression, a development for which I was immensely grateful. It was a relief to want to die again. In fact, in the months following my psychosis, suicidal ideation grew to be a sort of relief. When panic set in and I wondered if I was still going crazy, I'd just think, *Do I hate myself? Do I want to die?* The answer always came as a soothing yes.

———

In hindsight, I'm grateful for my psychosis. It took years, but eventually the trip came good. It was forty-five dollars well spent. My deep fear had always been becoming my father. I was convinced that if I wanted to not be like him, it would require constant vigilance in a never-ending, probably doomed war against myself. But in my psychosis, everything I had built for myself had collapsed and I had stood alone in the world, no constraints of civilisation, only my impulses and what I had thought was infinite liberty. I thought of the girl I'd sat opposite in the psych ward and how I'd thought about raping her. But I hadn't done it, a fact that undermined my fear of my own inherited evil.

At the same time, I had been initiated into the community of lunacy, and the experience lingered. My father had spoken of his 'illness' and for the first time I perceived what he might have meant. The annihilation of free will which fuses violence with innocence. I wondered, if a person believes life is a video game or a dream or that they're a representative of God, can you really consider them evil if they act accordingly? If I had done something awful while I'd been in the ward, how would I wish for the world to judge me? I hadn't – but what if I had? And ought I not apply the same thinking to my father?

I didn't know. All I knew was that something had changed. When I had swallowed the Hawaiian baby woodrose seeds something strange and vague had grown inside me: ambivalence.

Having sworn off illegal drugs and now any legal high, alcohol was the one remaining substance I felt didn't carry with it the risk of total craziness. It was the safe numbness.

I spent weekends drinking heavily with Greg, who looked like the wolf from *Little Red Riding Hood*, his face tapering impossibly in a lupine caricature, and Zed, a rotund babushka doll of a man with a chinstrap and a penchant for wearing jorts. Both were call-centre veterans in their early thirties. It was unclear if we were even friends, so steeped was our relationship in irony and sarcasm.

'I'm gonna slit your throat when you're sleeping, Kid,' Greg growled from behind his computer, and I laughed. The Kid was the nickname Zed and Greg had given me based on *Two and a Half Men*. I was the half-man, the kid, nearly a full decade younger.

'And I'm gonna come to your funeral and cut a swastika into your forehead,' added Zed.

We were a trinity of fucked-up man-children who believed in nothing, hoped for nothing. We were nihilists, but if any of us ever said that the other two would have called him a fuckhead. We listened to Nine Inch Nails on repeat and growled the lyrics like grimy clichés. All our fathers were shit and we joked about which of them would win in a rape contest. We vomited freely and laughed when we saw the spew on each other's shirts.

We embraced a shadow masculinity that thrived not on displays of strength or power but shows of sickness and self-destruction. To cough blood was courageous; to feel stabs of pain in your liver was valiant. The sicker you looked, the stronger you were.

We were making stories, memories. We had in-jokes, reminders of other times drinking ourselves into a stupor.

Between absolute commitment to never breaking the horrific characters we played, and the booze we drank, reality only existed when we passed out.

One day we went to Nimbin because Greg wanted pot. Zed drove Greg's blue car looking like a chubby trucker – his beard was brown as Christ's and flapped like a small albatross in the breeze blowing through the open windows. We stopped at each bottle shop we saw so we could get more beer for the road.

As we tore through sunlight-banged streets, we'd yell various forms of startling sentences at people, the weirder the better.

'Desire is the origin of all suffering!' we'd cry as a woman pushing a pram jerked her head up and glared at us.

A man with a topknot jumped four centimetres in the air when I screamed, 'We've given up too many liberties in the War on Terror!'

We drove from Sunday-slumbering Brisbane at around the time the morning church services end and people untuck their shirts and get stuck right back into sin. The road to Nimbin was paved with asphalt, then dirt, then mountains.

I'd never been to Nimbin. All I knew was it was in the mountains of northern New South Wales, and full of marijuana and people who aren't fond of suburbia, who hunger for the 'out' you always hear artists whisper about. That it was one of the places in Australia people go to get away from the middle-class pieces of shit.

The mountains were a banquet of life, miles and miles of indecipherable life. At one point I noticed a bee on the back seat beside me, just taking it easy. Even the bees up there knew how to luxuriate. I imagined living in the mountains with the bees and finding peace.

When we got there, though, Nimbin seemed wrong. It wasn't the Nimbin I had imagined, where shiny people shone because they were outlaws, free spirits, free thinkers, wild and intensely alive with glorious bodies for their wild and intensely alive souls. Instead, people shambled, the sun glowed pale like a sick junkie, dogs were motionless and mangy. Things were exactly as they appeared, there were no deeper levels, no gnostic curtains. Drug dealers were just drug dealers, nothing more. Where were the prophets, the poets, the holy stochastic encounters? Why was there what there was, and nothing more?

We saw a junkie sitting on a park bench and his eyes were rolling into the back of his head like wheels down into the valley of Death.

I turned to Greg and Zed. 'Jesus, this is the saddest place I've ever seen.'

Zed told me to stop whingeing. We were just here to get weed and then we'd go home. But I wasn't there for pot; I was there for the never-promised but always-expected oracles of my own hope. I wasn't there for the sadly rusting corrugated iron roofs, or the speed-ravaged teenage drug dealers with no mystery in their acne. I was there for Kerouac's mad ones.

We wandered around conspicuously until a thin, heroinish woman approached us offering 'treats'. She led Greg away to a backstreet. He returned with twenty-five dollars' worth of weed. The only problem was that he'd given her twice that. We laughed out of respect for the scam, got back into the car and headed home, away from the dirty, broken and addicted, the tatters of a failed revolution.

That trip was the endpoint of a certain type of self-destruction. I felt a last juvenile belief in the romance of chemicals crumble into dust. Salvation would not be found in intoxication, I realised at last.

11

Chloe came to a backpacker's hostel and saw me perform comedy.

I killed, and after my set I sat down at a table near her and her friends.

Chloe leaned across to me. 'That was great.'

'Um, thanks,' I mumbled. Despite performing stand-up comedy, receiving compliments made me about as comfortable as an agoraphobic in a mosh pit.

We watched the rest of the show together and once it had concluded, we kept chatting. I began to get the sense that she liked me, though I couldn't be sure. The fact that she had bought me several beers was a strong indicator but no guarantee. She kept laughing at every joke I made – but I was a comedian. I racked my brain for a way to indicate that I liked her while minimising the risk of being rejected in some humiliating fashion, such as her yelling, 'Mr White, I would sooner marry a sewage treatment plant than consider a romantic liaison with you.'

As luck would have it, one of her friends suggested a group photo to commemorate their night out. I stood while people crammed into the photo. Chloe rearranged several people, pushing her own brother from his position right beside me, so that she could stand there instead. I estimated there was a fifty per cent chance she liked me. I placed my arm around her and watched a smile spread across her face. Sixty per cent. She complimented the cologne I was wearing, and I ratcheted the probability up to seventy per cent.

As the English bartender struggled to take the photograph of our group, I leaned over and pressed my lips to Chloe's head. I was chuffed at my excellent, riskless choice.

At the end of the night, we got into a taxi and drove to Chloe's house. In the back seat we held hands and looked out the window, my stomach a butterfly enclosure. When the taxi pulled up, Chloe led me inside to her clean white bedroom scented with lavender. The bed was perfectly made.

'Nice room,' I said, thinking of my own dank room littered with beer bottles and empty casks of wine.

Chloe moved close and our lips met in softness.

We fell in love like the first cigarette after a long-haul flight. We trembled in delight from fulfilment.

It sounds awfully sentimental – because it *is* – but Chloe saved my life. Her tenderness was antibacterial; it cleaned the parts of me that felt I were too rotten for anyone else. She loved me and when she said she loved me I believed it, and when I said I loved her I believed it too. For the first time, I thought of somebody else as equal to or more important than myself. I understood why people said that love was like one heart in two bodies.

Chloe was from the complete opposite side of the tracks to me. Her mother was a piano teacher at a private school, while my mother probably stole pianos. Her father was a famous sports star, whereas my father was a rapist and not even a famous one.

I'd never been so happy. We lay in bed at night and talked ceaselessly until the birds sang the sun's ascent. Revealed every last one of our secrets. Cooked together; watched *The Sopranos* on her MacBook perched on one of the half-dozen cushions on her bed.

A glacier had become a river of life within me.

Someone loved me. *Me. She* loved me.

Equally amazing to me was that I loved her, because I had never loved anyone before. In fact, I'd harboured a secret fear that, really, I was a sociopath.

I researched recipes to cook for Chloe when she arrived home from university or work. Having lived mostly on instant noodles, these were abominably bad efforts. Brussels sprouts with salt and pepper, with a side of cold ham.

I bought chocolates and flowers for her, delighted by her delight.

Chloe had a wonderful, oddball sense of humour. She found the words 'pack', 'suit' and 'case' hilarious; if you said the sentence 'pack your suitcase' to her she'd keel over.

I adored the way she danced, how she swirled her hips and clicked her fingers in a deliberately daggy way. She didn't take things too seriously.

There were also some topics that she pursued with deadly seriousness, like her dreams. When we woke in the morning, usually the first topic of conversation was about a dream that she had.

We had been together for six months then twelve months. The future stretched out before us.

I didn't want to destroy myself any more. I wanted a life where I could love myself and those around me. I wanted to marry Chloe and buy a house and feast on the rich nectar of life. I wanted light. I had thought I wanted darkness, but I didn't. I hadn't had light and so I adapted to the dark, and over years of living in the darkness I thought the darkness was all I needed. But now I had light and I wanted everything to be covered with the light. There was still darkness but the light could resist it.

Chloe was the first person I had an orgasm with. I'd never ejaculated during sex, with men or women. Whenever I approached climax, I'd fixate on how long it was taking, the absurdity of myself as a thrusting naked ape. I'd cease being immersed in the moment and start thinking, *What if my heart explodes just right now? I could die. They must be hating this. Did my sweat just go in their eyes? Jesus Christ, why do I sweat so much? Eloi, Eloi, lama sabachthani.*

I'd say to my partner, 'Do you like this? We can stop if you want? If I was you, I'd want to stop.' I'd always tried to give the other person an orgasm and afterwards accepted the blue balls.

However, Chloe and I just fit. Our bodies worked. I came easily with her. I loved her smell, the colour of her skin, her nipples.

I even worked up the confidence to try dirty talking. Once, mid-coitus, I said to her, 'Your pussy feels so good.' She burst out laughing.

'What's funny?' I said, slipping sheepishly out of her.

'Pussy is such a gross word.'

'Well,' I sulked, 'what should I call it? Vagina is too clinical, cunt is too crass. I know! I'll call it a consent hole.'

She giggled. 'Oh yeah, baby, put your big cock in my consent hole.'

I laughed and rolled her into a hug.

'Just say you love me,' she murmured on my lips.

Why is there a bottle of wee on our wardrobe dresser?

I read the text from Chloe and winced.

It was there because her housemate Mia, who despised me, had been in the lounge room. Not wanting to risk interaction, I made the executive decision to piss in an empty Mount Franklin water bottle. I'd planned on taking it when I left the house but had forgotten.

I wanted her friends to like me but in my heart I knew they never would. It was my fault. I did no housework, only rarely washing dishes at Chloe's insistence. I was constantly sweating from hangovers. And, because I was now committed to making stand-up comedy a career, when they would try to open up a conversation, I'd usually quickly shut it down to go work on jokes.

I was selfish. When you can count on nothing but yourself, you tend to think of nothing but yourself.

I texted Chloe back, still wincing.

———

Slowly our tranquillity cracked. We became slower to forgive, quicker to anger. Where we used to laugh at our fights, now we clung to them. They festered from events into history.

On the other hand, comedy was going well. My material had matured somewhat, away from my needlessly aggressive rants against the evils of mandatory bike-helmet laws. I was becoming more interested in the little madness of being human. I felt able to connect to audiences in a new way. It wasn't that I was trying to take them to my point of view, but I was riffing on things that we had in common as human beings. I began to write about my experiences in the gay scene and with drugs. Between the personality obliteration of my psychosis and being in love, I just felt less angry inside, like I had less to prove.

A fast-rising comedian, Damien Power, had invited me to open for him at his 2012 Brisbane Comedy Festival show. I did well the whole week, and as I welcomed Damien on to the stage on the final night, he whispered in my ear, 'It's gonna be hard following you.'

After the show, a man came over and introduced himself to me, offering to buy me a drink. He was the booker for Sydney's Comedy Store, the most prestigious stand-up venue in Australia.

'I'd love to fly you down for some gigs,' he said over a beer.

'Cool,' I said, trying to disguise the volcano of joy inside me.

I started earning a little more money doing stand-up comedy, although still nowhere near enough to leave my part-time job at the call centre, or to feel financially secure.

Chloe wanted children and a house. I wanted those things too, though I was terrified I wouldn't be able to provide them. My biggest fear was Chloe and me ending up in our mid-thirties, me a bitter comic living on a shoestring, her an increasingly clucky, increasingly dissatisfied woman. I didn't want that for her. I'd sooner drive her to a speed dating evening to help her find a better man who could fulfil her dreams. 'You there, sir,' I'd cry like a bodhisattva cuckold, 'you seem better than I in every way. You should meet the love of my life.'

If I could succeed, though, I'd have the money to build the right future for us. I toyed with the idea of getting into commercial radio to get up enough money so we could buy a house.

As my comedy career progressed, I had to do more interstate travel, which meant when I was home I had to go to more open mics to work up material, which meant more time spent in libraries and cafes trying to write new jokes. My relationship with Chloe decayed.

I was simply not able to be a good partner. I had no money and a severe inability to regulate my own emotions. This was fine while I was single – I could spend days in bed – but in the context of an adult relationship, it was far from ideal.

She grew distant. We stopped being intimate. When I asked if something was wrong she insisted things were fine, she was just exhausted from working late-night bar shifts. I didn't raise the issue further.

I grew more suspicious, though, when, after finishing work at the bar, she wouldn't come home right away but often four or five hours later.

'I just went out with workmates,' she'd say.

It seemed strange that she was so exhausted from work but still could find the energy to go out drinking heavily after these shifts.

One afternoon, I was lying in bed reading when she came in to get something from one of her drawers. For the first time, I voiced my suspicion.

'Have you cheated on me?'

'No,' she said.

I didn't believe her and I repeated the question, 'Have you cheated on me? Please just be honest.' Something was deeply wrong.

She averted her eyes.

'Darling? Have you been cheating?'

She said no again, but didn't look up.

'Have you been cheating?'

She looked up, her eyes watering. The tears told me the answer, even before her mouth said, 'Yes.'

In an instant, my love for her transformed to hate.

'Fuck you,' I said. I looked at her, sunk to her knees, hands covering her face. 'How could you do this to me?'

'I'm sorry,' she whimpered into her palms.

I shuffled around her erratically, stuffing clothes and belongings into a suitcase. 'I loved you. I wanted to be with you forever.'

'I know. I didn't want to hurt you,' she said, crawling towards me across the carpet.

I stepped back from Chloe and beheld her, feeling my lip curl in disgust, willing it to twist even further with hate. 'How many times, how many men?'

'Only one,' she blubbered.

'Who was it?'

'The manager at my work.'

I thought of the late shifts she had been doing at the bar. I scolded myself for not trusting my intuition. I'd dismissed it as paranoia, a relic of life before Chloe, a mechanism in me which I had to learn to let go.

Chloe was now sobbing as she rocked on the spot.

I shivered with anger. 'How long?'

She stopped moving and was silent.

'Tell me,' I demanded.

'It doesn't matter.'

'The truth matters,' I spat.

'Six months,' she choked.

I stood silently as she kept saying that she was sorry, begging me to forgive her, that she hadn't meant to hurt me.

An anger I hadn't known since my childhood was working its way through me. It pulsed in my neck. I wanted to destroy her. To inflict unending damage, punish her for this betrayal. I could feel the weight of the suitcase in my hand. I dragged it behind me and stood over her. She looked up at me, puffy-eyed and red-faced.

I gathered all the venom, every bit of poison and hate and rage, into my mouth and spoke it. 'You are fucking disgusting.'

I turned my back on the sounds of her renewed disintegration, headed out the front door, suitcase in tow, onto the street.

'Hey,' I texted Chloe a few weeks later. 'Can we meet up and talk?'

She messaged back instantly. 'Yes we can.'

That Sunday we met in a park at the heart of the city.

'Is his dick bigger than mine?' I challenged Chloe for the seventieth time. I was genuinely concerned this was the root cause. Nothing to do with my emotional unavailability or financial dependence on her. I boiled such a complex, multifaceted thing as infidelity down to a question of penis dimensions.

I had to know everything about the other guy. What was his name? How old was he? What was his blood type? What did he think of Robert De Niro in *Goodfellas*? What was his star sign? His favourite colour? I asked the same questions I would if I were in love with him.

Absurdly, I tried to find positives in the situation. I told myself he had done me a favour by bringing the problems in our relationship to a head, that getting angry at him would be like getting angry at a pest inspector who discovers termites in your house.

We fell silent, drifting in our thoughts.

Staring at Chloe's pretty white legs as she adjusted them on the green grass, a pang of love tore me from my introspection. 'Are you okay?' I asked, thinking of her for the first time in the conversation.

She went to answer but tears streamed down her face. She opened up about the crushing pressure of being my partner, the burden of knowing that I had been hurt so much and that she was always conscious of never hurting me and now she had done just that. It had been hard for her, she cried, so hard. 'You're damaged, Corey, and I wanted to heal you, but I couldn't. It was too much for me.'

I hugged her. 'You gave me the only love I've ever had,' I sobbed. 'You did heal me, darling. You did.'

I felt oceanic shame at my blindness to the strain she'd laboured under. Trying to love me had depleted her. I felt repulsed by myself. I had loved her with all my heart. I had tried to be the best partner I could, and despite this, being with me had crushed Chloe, driven her to infidelity, reduced her to wet-cheeked angst in a public park.

I held her for a long while, her tears trickling through my shirt, wishing I had the power to change the two years we had been together.

By now the sun had dipped beneath the horizon and the air grew cold. We unhugged and Chloe rubbed her forearms. 'I should get going,' she said.

'I wish you wouldn't,' I replied. I didn't want her to go. I knew we were finished, that I could never trust her enough to be with her again. But looking at her sad, heart-shaped face, I wished that I could forever delay being apart forever.

She smiled faintly. 'I don't have to leave. You know, we could stay together, somewhere,' she suggested.

'Yes, we could,' I said in giddy collusion.

We couldn't go back to her house since her housemates would be there, nor to my friend's grandmother's place where I was crashing, but there was a hotel nearby.

The moment the door to our room shut behind us, we hopped in lust towards the couch, kicking our shoes off and flinging our clothes away between wild kisses. When at last we had stripped each other bare we collapsed onto the cream lounge. She scrambled atop me, hovering momentarily, looking down at me intensely. Then, wordlessly, she guided me inside her. We bucked together savagely without breaking eye contact. It was over in minutes.

Chloe got off me and showered. She emerged ten minutes later and I walked past her into the shower. When I came out she was sitting on the couch, hands crossed in her lap. I walked to her, the towel falling from my waist. I locked a swathe of her hair in my fingers and she went down on me briefly, before getting to her feet and pushing me backwards. I was temporarily frightened I'd trip and split my head open, but I let her guide me around a table and push me onto the bed.

We ordered room service. We slept. We lay down beside one another and stared into each other's eyes. We watched *Dr. Phil* and *The Bold and the Beautiful*. We held hands. We fucked in the shower, the tiles echoing our names. We left the hotel only once in three days, to buy a toothbrush and toothpaste. We had dozens of missed calls on our phones. We kept putting on the same clothes we'd been wearing since the park.

On the last night, lying in bed together in the dark, Chloe asked what the point of all this was. 'What are we doing?'

'Exploding apart,' I said melodramatically.

Chloe began sobbing and I started blubbering. We merged like frightened animals, shaking and weeping together.

When we had finished crying, she straddled me and leaned down, her brown hair enveloping me. Her lips met mine, bringing the salt of her tears.

The next morning's goodbye was a lingering hug. I tried to comfort Chloe.

'I want you to know that I'm okay, I don't want you to feel guilty, okay?'

Chloe nodded. 'I'm sorry.'

'I forgive you, okay?' I said, willing it into her eyes. 'And I'm sorry that I wasn't a better partner.'

'You did your best,' she said.

12

I decided to end my life by jumping off the Story Bridge. It sounds dramatic but how else can you kill yourself in Australia? Guns are too hard to acquire, sleeping pills are unreliable, and I never did Scouts so I don't know how to tie nooses. The only credible option was suicide by tall infrastructure.

I'd fallen into a deep depression since Chloe's infidelity and 15 October was the day I'd fixed in my calendar. There was no special significance to the date, I just wanted a few weeks to say goodbye to friends. I felt it would be rude to kill myself without one last coffee.

A paradox of suicide is that the time between deciding to do it and actually doing it is often filled with joy. Things glow because you're seeing them for the last time. The whole world becomes your deathbed and everything brims with meaning. It's like when you hand in your letter of resignation at a job you hate and the final few weeks don't seem that bad, so by the last day a part of you almost regrets leaving.

It's easy to see how this halo effect probably stops a lot of people from going through with it.

I, however, am not a quitter, and I gritted my teeth through the happiness spike.

I was twenty-five and I was done. All my past suicide attempts now seemed so juvenile and half-hearted. This time was different. I hadn't written a suicide note. This wasn't a cry for help, but an ingathering of silence.

I was contaminated, mutilated. For years I had believed that love held out the one hope of cleaning me and making me whole. Now I knew the truth. Love was just another way I'd wished in vain to be fixed. There was no salvific silver bullet. What was taken from me when I was young could not be replaced.

I walked along the bridge, cyclists and joggers whizzing and panting past me as ribbons of traffic flowed by. I stopped halfway, leaning over the barrier to gaze upon the Brisbane River seventy metres below. The water was black apart from a smear of moonlight that shimmered with the current. The light of apartments and offices speckled the skyline. People were going home to their people. A surge of self-pity rose up in me. I had been locked out of belonging, had tried to fight despite the odds. I had never belonged anywhere, though. I never had a chance. I didn't lose; I got beaten.

I pictured myself plummeting into the water which Google said height would make like concrete. I wondered what I'd think as I fell. Would I experience some titanic epiphany as my brain released DMT? Would my life flash before my eyes and make everything beautiful and holy?

Probably not. It didn't matter.

I'd half-expected a last-ditch atomic bomb of survival instinct to paralyse me, but instead there was only a feeling of resignation. The closer I got the easier it seemed. Why should I doubt something that felt so like destiny?

I stood for a few minutes savouring the finality.

I put my hands on the cool metal railing, prepared to kick up and over. This was the end of the thread of my life. This was how I didn't have to fight any more. Peace awaited.

Suddenly, the pocket of my jeans began vibrating. It took a few seconds for me to realise that it was my mobile phone. I didn't know why I'd brought it. I was going to kill myself – what did I need a phone for? To take a suicide selfie?

I dug it out of my pocket and saw a private number was calling. I answered: 'Hello?'

'Hello,' a woman replied. 'Am I speaking to Corey White?'

'Uh, yeah. Look, I'm sorry but I'm kind of busy at the moment.'

'That's okay, Corey. I just need to let you know this call will be recorded and monitored for quality and training purposes. Can I interest you in saving some money on your mobile phone bill?'

I burst out laughing, my body a cannon sending great cackling cannonballs ringing out in the darkness. I roared and gasped, doubled over, because I was about to save a lot of money on my mobile phone bill. My new plan would be pretty hard to beat: zero dollars for eternity.

I howled and shrieked at the sheer bleakness of my life. Everything had gone wrong: grew up in foster care, mother dead of a heroin overdose, father gone who knew where, raped, an ice addict, mentally ill, betrayed by the love of my life, and now, as I readied myself for suicide, a telemarketer had fucked that up too. I couldn't catch a break. If I leapt off the bridge, I'd probably land on a boat carrying mattresses.

Abruptly, I remembered the telemarketer on the other end of the line. 'Hello? Are you there?'

She was gone, understandably. There's only so long you can listen to a customer laugh maniacally before you have to accept the sale ain't gonna happen.

Serotonin, norepinephrine and dopamine – the whole neuro-chemical shebang – waterfalled through my body, ruining my suicidal mood.

I saw a doctor the next morning.

'What makes you think you're depressed?' he asked.

I thought about the improbable events of the night before. 'I'm just really sad.'

Half an hour later, I left his surgery clutching a prescription for Lexapro.

I'd always been suspicious of antidepressants. My gut instinct was that Big Pharma was pathologising the human condition. Wasn't it normal for people to feel sad? To yearn for the plane they were on to crash? To wear a chicken skeleton as a hat and petition the Blood God for death?

All that now seemed hollow. I was pathological – I did need to be cured.

Empty too was my old fear that antidepressants were too dangerous to take. I'd been a drug addict. I'd shelved MDMA, snorted cocaine, sniffed amyl in a Holden Barina driven by a man smoking a bong *as he drove*, smoked ice for days until my gums bled and the blood dribbled down onto my shirt. If antidepressants were crazier than any of those drugs, my dealers would have sold them to me.

Taking Lexapro might mean turning a corner. They could be the beginning of recovery. I couldn't count on a Filipino telemarketer to save me again.

Within a month, the pills started to work. Depressed thoughts still strolled around my skull but at a more leisurely pace, taking iced tea under umbrellas. Present yet bearable, like turning the volume down on a Nickelback song.

It wasn't all sunshine and lollipops, though – the Lexapro came with side effects. Now my orgasms felt how tofu tastes, the prospect of ejaculating no more erotic than a photograph of a brick. I tried masturbating out of detached curiosity and felt nothing except that I was wasting time and toilet paper, the latter of which I now needed for my newly acquired perpetual and vicious diarrhoea.

Nevertheless, I felt fantastic, and I kicked myself for not taking medication years ago.

'You have to get on Lexapro,' I evangelised to anyone who'd ever frowned in front of me. All of them politely fobbed me off, but I didn't mind.

———

Shortly after the serendipity of the bridge, I moved to Melbourne, into a ramshackle Californian bungalow with an old comedian friend and a middle-aged indie singer. In summer, the sun beat down severely on the house, slowly cooking all inhabitants. When I finally managed to fall asleep at night I tossed and turned, dreaming I was a potato roasting in an oven.

After the telemarketer's grace, my commitment to comedy had deepened. Conventional wisdom held that Brisbane was a backwater with no promise of advancement beyond a few meat-grinder clubs and, if you were bland enough, dreaded cruise ships. If you wanted to be a real comedian then you had to go to Melbourne, Australian comedy's mecca. All roads led to this clown Rome, the glitzy, pulsating heart of show business, home to a prestigious international comedy festival every April.

So I moved there, eschewing employment in favour of going on the dole so that I could concentrate 100 per cent on comedy.

I was so poor I stole individual cashews from my housemates. In the dead of night I tiptoed to the kitchen and, in the stripe of the fridge's light, knife in hand, I carved the thinnest slice I could from one of their blocks of cheese. I went into the pokies areas of pubs for free coffee and biscuits. Even with an elderly woman crying on a Queen of the Nile machine beside me, it was still better than working in call centres.

Sometimes I ran out of antidepressants and couldn't afford to refill my prescription until my next dole payment. In the meantime, I would spend days battling dizziness, brain zaps and sporadic spasms in my arm or leg. Once, my friend Luka was driving me home from a gig. I hadn't taken my medication in nearly a week and was curled up in withdrawal. Suddenly, a wave of nausea galloped up through me. 'Can you stop the car?' I said, too late. A little jet of vomit bubbled out of my mouth onto my shirt.

My room resembled one in a halfway house for parolees. The only furniture it contained was a bed, a chair I'd borrowed from our kitchen and a desk I'd found on the side of the road. It reeked too, since I was chain-smoking and surviving mostly on a diet of black coffee and cups of white rice drenched in sweet chilli sauce.

I was so poor I was reduced to scavenging for change. I hunted beneath the couch cushions, in my drawers, lifted furniture up and down, praying there was money somewhere. I looked at the back of the freezer, in the oven, climbed onto the roof.

One afternoon, I emerged with $2.80 in five-cent coins and headed to buy a bottle of milk. I dropped the shrapnel onto the counter at the grocery store and said to the shopkeeper, 'Sorry about the change.' He looked at me unimpressed. I smiled like someone strapped to an electric chair, except instead of electricity I was dying of shame. He grunted and swept the little mountain of coins into the till.

When you're poor you notice things you never would if you had money, and I noticed he had accepted the mound of five-cent coins without counting them. As I walked home, I entertained the possibilities of this new insight. Could I save money by going into a shop and paying in five-cent pieces and so take advantage of people's laziness? I would start small and only cheat them out of five cents at first. If that worked, I would graduate to underpaying by ten cents. Then fifteen, twenty or fifty cents! I had a supremely useless but wonderful thought: *If I ever need to pay a ransom, I'm going to pay it in five-cent coins.* I laughed very hard at the idea. Maybe it was just the loopy nadir of poverty, maybe it was the fact I had not eaten vegetables in months, but I was tickled by the idea of trying to assure a bandit in a balaclava that sixty wheelbarrows filled with five-cent coins did add up to a million dollars.

'There's a million if you count it. Pinky promise. Can I have my wife back, please?'

At home, I pilfered my housemates' used cigarettes from ashtrays on the porch and in the lounge room. I'd brush their charred ends off searching for brown, unsmoked tobacco. If I straightened the butt mangled from being crushed after being smoked, they were usually good for a few drags, enough nicotine to quell my cravings.

When Melbourne's biting winter arrived I had no warm clothes so I spent whole days lying in bed beneath my doona. I fretted about developing a blood clot and every hour I'd spring from my thermal sanctuary to jog on the spot, kicking my knees up as high as possible like a cyclist on an invisible bike, to drive blood through my body, before diving back into my warm cocoon.

Despite the financial sacrifices I was making, my career in comedy wasn't going as well as I had hoped. I began to question whether this was what I should be doing with my life. How much longer could I go on living like this?

I made a bargain with myself. The 2015 Melbourne International Comedy Festival was nine months away and I decided I'd do a show. It would be my first solo stand-up show, to be called *The Cane Toad Effect*. If it went well then I would keep going with comedy. If not, then perhaps I could return to university.

I knew that I wasn't as broadly funny or friendly or photogenic as other comedians. I could only do the sort of comedy that I found funny. I could never be them, no matter how hard I tried. I could only be myself. Sometimes when I performed I had this acidic sense of being a great black cloud ruining an otherwise joyous evening of comedy, with my talk of mental illness or foster care, but I hoped there was an audience out there that would get it and me.

This was how I wrote *The Cane Toad Effect*. As the kind of show I would like to see and as the only show I could write. Out of despair and a fuck-it attitude, as if it might be my first and last.

When I was ten, my mother died of a heroin overdose, which sounds sad but at least she died doing what she loved.

It was a terrible hack joke I soon discarded, but it sparked the rest of the show, which I wrote virtually in its entirety during one long manic week.

I wanted to say something important with my show, I wanted to share what I believed. And what did I believe? I hoped to find out by trying to say it.

Before I opened at Melbourne Comedy Festival, I did a run at the Sydney Fringe Festival. Audiences came, reviewers were kind – it was the best I could have hoped for. Or so I thought.

Poverty answers the phone in a particular way. When the Sydney Fringe organisers called to tell me I'd won the award for Best Comedy Show, I answered like someone in witness protection.

'Hello,' I said, dawdling out the front of my house.

'I was looking to speak with Corey. Is this Corey?'

'It's, uh, Corey's phone. What do you want?'

'I'm Chris from the Sydney Fringe. I'm looking to speak with Corey White. Is this Corey?'

'Oh, hey, man. Yeah, it's me, Corey.'

'Why did you say it was *Corey's phone?*'

'I've got some issues with debt collectors,' I explained. I'd drained every line of credit available to me in order to finance the move to Melbourne, the repayments on which I'd subsequently defaulted on.

Chris laughed. 'I'm calling to let you know that the judges have decided your show was the best comedy show of the Sydney Fringe. Congratulations.'

'Wow.'

'It was really fantastic,' he said. 'Very funny, very moving.'

Feeling sheepish, I asked whether the award came with a cash prize.

'Oh no,' he said, 'but there is a beautiful certificate you can collect next time you're in Sydney.'

'Sounds great,' I sighed cheerily.

I thanked him for the call and we hung up. I pushed my mobile back into my pocket. It was at this very moment that a button on my pants shot off into the grass. They were one of only two pairs of pants I owned, purchased from a second-hand store for a steal. Recovering that button was vital. Unable to find it in the overgrown lawn, I replaced it with a safety pin, which for the next few weeks consistently popped undone if I walked too quickly or exhaled too forcefully, sending my pants slowly sliding down my award-winning legs.

The Sydney Fringe award, while a confidence boost, was relatively unimportant. It didn't alter a looming problem facing me, namely the approaching deadline for registering for the upcoming Melbourne festival. This was a proposition requiring a substantial financial investment I hadn't figured out how to deal with.

Fortunately, Jake, who had first booked me for the Sydney Comedy Store, called to tell me they were prepared to produce *The Cane Toad Effect* in Melbourne.

They would cover all costs. They believed in the show.

I was elated, and as Jake drilled down into details I commenced a silent and joyous one-man waltz through my house, shimmying out of my room, whirling through the hallway, pirouetting into the lounge then leaping like a ballerina through the doorway into the kitchen.

'We'll talk more soon,' Jake said, wrapping up the call.

'Yes,' I replied, extending my arm above my head theatrically, waggling my hips like a maniac.

This was my chance. I climbed back into bed and carefully opened my laptop, with its broken screen hanging onto the keyboard by a single hinge, and pored over the text of *The Cane Toad Effect*. I had to make it perfect.

Six months later I commenced my first-ever Melbourne Comedy Festival run and brought down the house. Word spread that *The Cane Toad Effect* was worthy of watching. Audiences and comedians flooded in. Show after show sold out, extra performances were added and those sold out too.

Reviewers praised it, citing it as a potential candidate to win the Best Newcomer Award, bestowed on the debut show judges deemed the finest. I tried not to think about the award. Obviously, winning would advance my career enormously. Honestly, though, I was more excited about the fact shows were selling out because this meant I was making money, which meant I'd be able to buy fresh, previously unsmoked cigarettes, nice juicy steak, clothes with that new sweatshop smell.

After I'd performed two dozen shows over the month, the evening arrived when the award winners would be announced. Nominees for all categories were invited to an exclusive pre-awards gathering in a room above the theatre where the ceremony would take place. For an hour, we mixed nervously in an atmosphere heavily pregnant with anxiety, over-smiling at those with whom we were in competition, engaging in pleasant chitchat with nominees in other categories.

I planted myself at one food table, gorging myself on party pies, salmon blinis and feta-stuffed mushrooms. Below us, the venue filled with attendees.

The ceremony began and I headed downstairs to stand at the back of the cavernous room, thronged by comedian friends, holding a can of Melbourne Bitter which I sipped every few nanoseconds.

Festival honchos made official remarks and thanked sponsors, audiences, support staff, comedians and the concept of laughter.

Slowly, they announced the winners of various awards – best independent production, the people's choice award. Victors took to the stage, gave thanks, posed for an official photograph before descending back into the crowd.

Finally, it was time to announce the winner of the Best Newcomer Award. The host read the names of the nominees to rounds of applause.

'It gives me great pleasure to announce that the winner of this year's Best Newcomer Award is . . . Corey White.'

I heard the roar, felt it move through my body as I was being shaken like a rag doll by everyone around me. I hugged my friends Kevin and Mitch, who whispered their pride into my ringing ears. Half-blind from tears, I jogged through the crowd and onto the glowing stage.

I thanked my management, the staff at my venue, friends who had loaned me money to stay afloat, my friend John for getting me into comedy. I ended my speech, sensing my throat was on the verge of flooding. I posed for a photograph then floated off the stage in a daze, back through the crowd of people grinning with raised thumbs

In my life, meaning has been like lightning, not electricity. It has flashed and vanished. That night was a million lightning bolts striking the earth at once. I thought about my mother and father, the cockroaches, psych wards, Tracey and her son Matt, the long years of loneliness, Chloe, the Story Bridge and the grace that yanked me out of night. The totality of it all had led me to here. Suffering, madness, hope and blind luck had guided me through time to this moment. No matter what happened in the future, I would try to hold on to this feeling.

In the early hours of the morning, I stumbled out of a taxi and bumbled across my front lawn drunk and happy, a half-eaten kebab in one hand and a second kebab in the other. I wolfed the first down as I struggled for several minutes to open the front door. Once inside, I dropped the spare kebab beside my bed for when I woke up.

Someone had gifted me a packet of cigarettes as congratulations. I wandered out to the backyard, slid one from the packet and lit it. I took a long drag, breathed the smoke out and gazed up at the faded stars in the last of the night.

13

The glory of winning Best Newcomer was fragile. Praise brought the fear of losing praise. What would I do next? How could I follow up? Existence without acclaim seemed impossible to endure now.

People and room runners and media who never would have given me the time of day before now fell over themselves to offer me gigs and opportunities, to strike up conversations. It was like my success had gone to other people's heads, as if they thought that proximity to me would translate to success for them. It wasn't fame, more the social magnetism of a man who has won a meat raffle in a country pub. It seemed everybody was angling for a lamb chop.

Offers of stand-up appearances came from around the country, the ABC wanted me to make a television show, and I was asked to appear on *Australian Story*. I said yes to the avalanche, even as I felt snowed under by it, because I was frightened of plummeting back into poverty and anonymity.

My agreeing to appear on *Australian Story* was primarily political.

I wanted to use my tiny profile to raise awareness of the injustices in the foster care system, which have been completely ignored by broader society. I felt it was my duty.

Of course, I was naive. All that happened was I briefly became a sort of inspiration-porn star. People messaged, texted and emailed me telling me how brave I was. But the machine that generated my suffering was still devouring children. The foster care system remained out there, an architecture of suffering impervious to the earnestness of a nano-celebrity.

At the behest of the producers, I contacted my father to see if he would appear on the episode.

His speech was glacial, apparently from medication, but I figured more likely alcohol and illegal drugs. I could tell the years had beaten the shit out of him.

'I do stand-up comedy now, Dad.' I felt strange saying *Dad*. I hadn't said it out loud for over a decade.

'You were always funny, Corey. Do you remember when I took you to the Brisbane Ekka and on the train home you kept asking me why starving people in India don't just eat the cows? Everyone in the carriage laughed.'

'No, I don't remember, sorry.'

'We were coming home from the Ekka and you had all your showbags and we had a great day.'

'I guess I was too young.'

'You were six or seven.'

We went back and forth, me quickly, him slowly, until I arrived at the point of the call. After I asked him, he fell silent.

'I don't think that'd be a good idea.'

'Okay,' I said.

I wasn't angry at him. I saw him clearly, as a man who had fled from the truth his whole life. He was an animal once dangerous, now in the twilight of its power.

He slurred, 'I don't want to go on the show,' for the fifth or sixth time.

'I understand, Dad. Well, I better go.'

'I love you, Corey.'

His declaration froze me. The desperation in it was sickening. I felt the power I had over him. It occurred to me that I could annihilate him with a sentence, even silence. I closed my eyes. 'I love you too, Dad.'

I toured *The Cane Toad Effect* for months around Australia then Edinburgh and London. By the end the words felt absurd, meaningless. The truth bled out, the authenticity frittered away in mechanical repeats. The machinery of my mind began to break down. When I wasn't performing, I lay in bed staring blankly at the ceiling.

I thought of suicide constantly. Something was erupting in me, something was coming for me, from deep within, which I couldn't overcome or avoid or bust through with laughter. A force and shape which I realised *The Cane Toad Effect* skimmed over superficially, maybe even disingenuously.

I could no longer outrun my past. It had finally arrived to rip me apart.

A nervous breakdown. It was the annihilation of all the armour I'd built for myself over a lifetime.

I broke into sobbing fits randomly. I'd go into disabled toilets, turn off the lights and lie in the foetal position to shake and moan, crying until there was a knock on the door, at which point I wiped my eyes and plodded out past a disgruntled man in a wheelchair.

I was more tired than I'd ever been, and my body was in constant pain. My muscles ached, twitching at random intervals. I'd go days without sleeping. I found it hard to speak. I couldn't remember words.

And all through this, torrential injunctions in my skull to kill myself, go on, do it.

I was admitted to a psychiatric hospital after forming a plan to jump in front of a train after tweeting 'Goodbye' along with a YouTube link to 'The Gambler' by Kenny Rogers. After a few days, and drawing on my previous psych ward experience, I lied my way out, conditional on my seeing a psychiatrist.

'I think you have Complex Post-Traumatic Stress Disorder,' said the psychiatrist.

'What's that?'

'You've heard of Post-Traumatic Stress Disorder.'

'Yes.'

'Well, Complex Post-Traumatic Stress Disorder is a more complex form of that.'

'Okay,' I said, still not understanding.

He explained that PTSD was a psychological response to an overwhelming danger. Soldiers developed it, as I knew, after traumatic incidents. Complex PTSD developed after multiple, repeated traumatic incidents, especially ones a person couldn't escape from.

On the bus home from the session, I read the entry for C-PTSD on Wikipedia, which said:

> Complex post-traumatic stress disorder (C-PTSD; also known as complex trauma disorder) is a psychological disorder that can develop in response to prolonged, repeated experience of interpersonal trauma in a context in which the individual has little or no chance of escape. C-PTSD relates to the trauma model of mental disorders and is associated with chronic sexual, psychological or physical abuse or neglect in childhood, chronic intimate partner violence, victims of kidnapping and hostage situations, indentured servants, victims of slavery and human trafficking, sweatshop workers, prisoners of war, concentration camp survivors and defectors of cults or cult-like organizations. Situations involving captivity/entrapment (a situation lacking a viable escape route for the victim or a perception of such) can lead to C-PTSD-like symptoms, which include prolonged feelings of terror, worthlessness, helplessness, and deformation of one's identity and sense of self.

I struggled to smother a rising sense of optimistic identification. The article continued:

- Difficulties regulating emotions, including symptoms such as persistent dysphoria, chronic suicidal preoccupation, self-injury, explosive or extremely inhibited anger (may alternate), or compulsive or extremely inhibited sexuality (may alternate).

- Variations in consciousness, including forgetting traumatic events (i.e., psychogenic amnesia), reliving experiences (either in the form of intrusive PTSD symptoms or in ruminative preoccupation), or having episodes of dissociation.

- Changes in self-perception, such as a chronic and pervasive sense of helplessness, paralysis of initiative, shame, guilt, self-blame, a sense of defilement or stigma, and a sense of being completely different from other human beings.

- Varied changes in the perception of the perpetrator, such as attributing total power to the perpetrator (though the individual's assessment of power realities may be more realistic than the clinician's), becoming preoccupied with the relationship to the perpetrator, including a preoccupation with revenge, idealization or paradoxical gratitude, seeking approval from the perpetrator, a sense of a special relationship with the perpetrator or acceptance of the perpetrator's belief system or rationalizations.

- Alterations in relations with others, such as isolation and withdrawal, persistent distrust, anger and hostility, a repeated search for a rescuer, disruption in intimate relationships and repeated failures of self-protection.

- Loss of, or changes in, one's system of meanings, which may include a loss of sustaining faith or a sense of hopelessness and despair.

- Disconnection from surroundings accompanied by feelings of terror and confusion.

Reading these symptoms, I finally understood the appeal of horoscopes. These symptoms defined me. Through them I could decipher the world and myself.

That I had issues was an understatement on par with 'Gee whiz, that Idi Amin was an unpleasant feller.' But the satisfyingly crisp objectivity of a diagnosis meant I was no longer in a morass of untethered, shifting feelings and moods.

I read all that I could find on the subject, connecting the dots between the dry clinical jargon and myself.

Complex PTSD isn't a mental illness. It is in many ways an ossified rational response to trauma. Those who've experienced childhood trauma have a faulty amygdala, the part of the brain that regulates threat via the fight-flight mechanism. It's like having a fire alarm in your house that goes off when you boil the kettle or someone lights a cigarette two streets over.

C-PTSD is also a disorder of time. It destroys linearity. It shatters chronology. One of its defining features are emotional flashbacks. These transport you to traumatic childhood experiences, except there's no sight or sound, just the emotions of what you felt as a child. Eschatological terror, rage, shame and humiliation so thick your throat closes up and you forget who you are. It's like a time machine in your head, only you can't control it.

Until I was diagnosed, when people spoke of the power of being labelled I dismissed it as platitudinous. Now I understood. To be labelled meant your pain was patterned and therefore predictable. It could be controlled and fought against as others had controlled and fought against it. I was no longer alone. Instead I belonged to a great mass of the similarly tormented and there was comfort in this. I was not an exile, but one of many.

This was what I'd been chasing all these years. At last I had found the truth of my life.

True to my lifelong form, however, this was itself a sort of salvation fantasy.

Diagnosis of my condition did nothing to improve it. I was like an oncologist with cancer. Things I knew intimately destroyed me despite my knowledge.

My mind was nothing but a carousel of cruelties: *kill yourself, kill yourself, kill yourself.* A flood of grim visions assailed me in the days and the nights, inner sights so macabre they make me laugh now, like the time I walked past a construction site and thought about jumping in the hole and burying myself alive, imagining my hand scooping one last handful of dirt on top before patting flat the earth around it.

I slept for days or I went days without sleep. I broke out in a rash; patches of my hair fell out. Paranoia took hold of me and I didn't leave the house for days. When I did, it was to walk to the pub and drink more quickly than I ever had before.

It went on and on.

I lay curled in bed one afternoon, self-hatred eating me up.

I hate you, I hate you, I hate you. You piece of shit.

The words seemed to come from some other entity inside me.

Exhausted and delirious, I spoke back to it. *Why do you hate me? Please just tell me.*

There was a pause inside my skull.

Somehow I knew that voice was me, my younger self. Snarling through time and space, wounded and alone.

The voice said, *I don't know.*

You're hurt, aren't you? I asked it.

It didn't reply.

You're hurt, aren't you?

The voice didn't say anything, but I sensed its vitriol diminish.

I began to talk to the voice over the following days whenever thoughts of loathing arose. The more I did, the more I was convinced it was me, as a child.

A stream of memories and feelings began to flow from him. Old recollections I believed I had made my peace with now flashed in my mind's eye, fresh nightmares fully felt. He was showing me his terror and confusion, ignored and minimised for so long. I felt sorrow at the evil.

Gradually, the presence inside me ceased to radiate hate and hurt. He was being acknowledged.

Then an extraordinary thing happened. Sympathy began to also flow from him to me. For the ways I had mutilated myself for over a decade. For my desperate hunger for love, which I had tried to feed with drugs and alcohol. The weeks and months and years of isolation. Christmases alone, and New Year's Eves alone, birthdays unmarked by anyone outside of a text message from my sister Rebecca. The addiction, the depression. The loneliness that withered me.

He understood me, because he was me. He had been with me in the drug dens, in the call centres, in the madness.

For weeks, I spoke to him constantly, out loud. Something elemental was being restored. I was being renewed. All pain vanished from my body, the rashes disappeared, I slept better than I ever had.

I began reading about the inner child, how our personalities are the fossilised reactive patterns of our younger selves designed to ensure our survival, and all the fucked-up parts of us at one time were our protection. My inner child had carried me through the years. He had survived, withstood the horror, for me. I originated from him. He was my father and my mother.

I love you, I said to him over and over.

The literature advocated crying as a way to come home to your inner child and heal them. I embraced this project wholeheartedly. I sought out the saddest movies: *Requiem for a Dream*, *Schindler's List*, *Boys Don't Cry*, *Philadelphia*, *Inside Out*, *Up*. I blubbered so much I considered seeking a sponsorship deal with Kleenex.

These tears were different to any I'd shed before. They were healing. I cried for myself, for the childhood taken from me. I wept for the brutality inflicted on a little boy and how he had preserved that brutality inside himself, becoming its fiercest advocate. I sobbed about the adulthood which resulted from all this, the wounds to identity and trust which might never heal.

Wherever I went, I paid attention to the child inside me. When he felt frightened, I told him he was safe now. When he felt ashamed, I told him he was acceptable. When he felt angry, I told him he was allowed to be.

I told him about who he would be when he grew up. I told him about Chloe. I told him he would become a stand-up comedian and he would make thousands of people laugh. He would perform at the Opera House. He would travel on planes across the world. He would have money and be able to buy food whenever he wanted. He would even have sex!

His happiness grew.

It was a long day of the soul. A sunburst of nurturing myself after so many years of self-flagellation and disgust. How can I convey my gratitude for the coup de grace of total breakdown which delivered me wounded and shivering to myself? How a broken man was healed by the child he was?

I read about 're-parenting': mentally travelling back to traumatic experiences and intervening as an adult to rescue your younger self. You restored justice, which would soothe your inner child.

I intervened in every terrible memory: I confronted my father, my mother, Tracey, Matt, anyone who had ever hurt me. In memory after memory, I arrived to protect myself, to rescue him. Each time I did, I felt lighter, airier, more whole.

One afternoon, sitting in a park smoking a cigarette, I knew there was only one more journey to be made. I'd read case notes during the filming of *Australian Story* of the first time I had been placed in foster care. A social worker from the Department had found me as an eight-month-old alone in a caravan. My parents had abandoned me to score drugs, and I was left there, without food and water, for days.

I closed my eyes against the sun and went back to myself as a baby, in that caravan.

I walked through a caravan park on the outskirts of a grimy, rundown town. I approached a beat-up white caravan. Inside it was dark and hot, littered with empty beer bottles and cans of rum. I saw a baby in a cot, eerily silent. He had given up; nobody had come when he had wailed.

I reached down and picked up the noiseless, pale baby and held him to my chest.

I could smell my tears flowing to my lips.

I comforted the baby, told him everything was okay, as I fixed a bottle for him to drink. I whispered over and over, 'I love you, I love you, I love you.'

Even as I said those words, rage was baking my throat dry.

How could you do this to a baby? How could you do this to your own flesh and blood? How could my parents have transgressed like this? I was glad my mother was dead, glad my father was old and broken.

I gazed at the baby and my anger died down. He had my mother's eyes, brown and unfathomably deep, and my father's nose, broad and flat. I didn't know what I felt any more. Something between fury and forgiveness, a no-man's land dividing love and hate.

I still perceive my inner child inside me. Every now and then I sense self-hatred well up in him, but I project love and compassion. I tell him that we are safe, that he has no reason to hate himself or me. I feel him quieten, sense his loathing and loneliness fade. I rarely talk to him out loud like I did in those first odd weeks. It is not necessary; we understand one another, we are happy in our wordlessness. He knows that I love him, that I care for him.

He and I are not fully healed. I don't know if a final healing is possible. Throughout my life I have searched for epiphanies and salvation to fix me. I look back and see how I tried to find meaning in academia, intelligence, sexuality, drugs, nihilism, romance and comedy, thinking every time each would be the thing that saved me. I clawed and clung to them hoping they would decontaminate me, make me real, worthwhile. They never could. Because it is not people or objects that saved me, but my hunger for them, which lay inside me. My relentless wish for salvation was my salvation.

What happens inside me nowadays seems gentler and less turbulent. It sounds so awfully cheesy, but I love myself.

I try to keep the peace with those parts of myself that only want war, to hurt myself, that see romance in self-destruction. Because really there is no other way. They cannot be defeated. They will always be part of me. Everything in me had a purpose, once. The desire for self-destruction was a warped desire to escape pain. The desire to turn away from people and focus only on one thing as the sole hope was a desire to escape cruelty and ensure safety. Beneficent Darwinian behaviours, wisdom that defied terror. They are not a sickness, but healthy survival mechanisms grown old.

I still have difficult days and weeks, but I no longer feel as though I'm lacking something fundamental. What I once regarded as a void is now a serenity. The love I gave my inner child in those months of solitary mystic communion filled it in.

To feel that love, to love him like that, to be loved by him like that, was all I'd ever wanted. It penetrated deeper than anything else could ever reach. It was and is a love so true that it requires no faith. It cannot be betrayed, broken or taken. It was there at the beginning, will be there at the end. And I know that even when I lie down in bed for a few days in apocalyptic despair, and I do not know who I am, and I doubt the goodness of every atom of the world, I still know that this love resides in me like a sun, unceasing and powerful, immune to time, untouched by suffering, invincible.

Epilogue

I wake up. *Where am I? What's happening?*

The fear dissipates when I realise I'm home in bed with Sophie.

We're getting married soon. She is smart, funny, beautiful and kind. Weddings are expensive so we're saving, but I'm kind of glad we have to wait because I'm a little overweight and look like a professional darts player. This delay gives me time to get into shape.

Sophie is snoring – what she calls her 'purring', a cute euphemism for a lawnmower inches from my head.

I sense something behind me and I twist to look. Spread out against the wall is a silhouette, of a man hanging in a noose. It's huge, iconographic, implying some inverse relationship to the image of the Crucifixion.

Have I done something wrong? Is this a message from my subconscious? I have been so focused on work lately. I dream of a day when we will have enough money to buy a house, in the country with a little bit of land. I wish I could be more productive.

My mind whirs with anxiety as I stare at the looming figure. Am I going crazy? Why am I seeing this? What if I snap and kill Sophie in my sleep? What if the blood of my father somehow contorts my body into some murderous pattern? Should I run out of the house to keep her safe?

And I know what is happening. I am going back in time again, flashing back to previous terror. It has happened so many times before – but now I reject it.

I draw away from the dark shadow emblazoned metres from me and look at Sophie. She is real and ordinary, pale in the moonlight. Her mouth is comically agape, nose awkwardly vertical, forehead glossy from her bedtime shower. Seeing her like this makes me feel especially tender towards her.

I think of how many years I'll get to spend with her, and gratitude blooms in me to the point I want to wake her up and blurt out how lucky I feel. But I don't.

Instead I gently entangle my legs with hers, the way she asks me to do each night as we doze off. And I drift to sleep this way, mingled with the woman I love, who is now snoring quite loudly, my back turned on shadows of supposed revelation.

Acknowledgements

A massive thank you to my brilliant, long-suffering editor Cate Blake. I could not have written this book without your skill, patience, vision, wisdom and humour. You took a rambling, sloppy manuscript and helped me turn it into a book. Witnessing the miracles you worked with a tweak here and line break there has been astonishing. It has taken longer than it should have, but we got there. Thank you for enduring.

Thank you to everyone at Penguin Random House. In particular, Lou Ryan for organising the literary salons and numberless other things, Clive Hebard for editing the manuscript with the eye of an eagle, Bella Arnott-Hoare for being a PR wizard and Adam Laszczuk for designing a beautiful cover. A special thank you to Nikki Christer, Group Publishing Director, for your kindness and interest, which boosted my spirits more than you can know.

Thank you to Kevin Whyte, head of Token and the Dumbledore of Australian comedy. You made me feel believed in – because of you

I continued marching. I am eternally indebted to you for taking time out of your hectic schedule to read drafts and resolve my circular worries. Thank you also to my manager Sam Gray, for your tireless work and words of encouragement.

Thank you to the friends who assisted with the manuscript or listened to me ramble down the phone line in despair/mania. To James Masters, for your careful appraisal of the first few chapters and your encouragement to go on. Thank you for making me laugh at my own seriousness. To Alex Senior, for your thoughtful feedback, unrelenting support and your chain-smoking disquisitions. I owe you several tonnes of cigarettes. To James McCann, for being a genius. Your erudition and ceaseless optimism helped me see the bigger picture. Whenever I spoke with you about the writing, I always came away inspired and ready to jump back into it.

Thank you to Mitch Alexander. Though life has conspired to keep us both extraordinarily busy recently, I remember fondly when we had longer conversations (arguments) more often. You helped me so much when I was down, for which I will always be grateful.

Thank you to Kevin Lim, for being good and honest. Your grouchiness, loyalty and big heart are very precious to me.

Thank you to Rose Callaghan, for your energy that helped get the book over the line when I thought I couldn't go on.

Thank you to Tom Sanderson, for many things.

Thank you to Sameena and Mike, for your friendship and tenderness in troubled times as things all came to a head.

Thank you to my sisters Jacinta White, Rebecca Van Tienhoven and Belinda Gambrill. Slowly restoring our relationships has been one of the great joys of my life.

Lastly, thank you to Sophie Jenkins, to whom this book is dedicated. I'm a lucky pot of dirt to have a flower like you in my life. Thank you for weathering the madness of writing a book, for putting up with my crankiness, weariness and long stares into the middle distance. Thank you also for your valuable notes on the manuscript when you were tired from your own work. I love you, let's go on a nice long holiday.